Romania's rocky road
from the Ceaușescu dictatorship to fragile democracy

Appendix: Reports of 31 former students
of the Babeș-Bolyai University in Cluj-Napoca/Romania
who live today in Romania and abroad

by Prof. Dr. Dr. Johannes Kneifel

Translation:
From German into American-English by
DeepL

Engelsdorfer publishing house
Leipzig
2023

This book is not a scientific work, but a personal experience report about Romania.

Prof. Dr. Dr. Johannes Kneifel
Born 1939

Bibliographic information provided by the German National Library:
The German National Library lists this publication in the German National Bibliography; detailed bibliographic data are available on the Internet at https://dnb.de.

ISBN 978-3-96940-468-3
Copyright (2023) Engelsdorfer Verlag Leipzig
All rights by the author
Cover image © Björn Wylezich [Adobe Stock]
Made in Leipzig, Germany (EU)
Printed on FSC® certified paper
www.engelsdorfer-verlag.de
14,80 Euro (D) – 13,30 GBP (UK) – 16,00 USD (USA)

The Marquis de Custine wrote
in the 19th century after a trip to Russia:

„Oppressed peoples always deserve their punishment -.
Tyranny is the work of nations,
not the masterpiece of one individual."

The writer Panait Istrati wrote
1929 after a 16-month trip to the Soviet Union:

„The real drama of my life and writing career was born in the USSR. There I saw how compact masses – not individual tyrants – are capable of tyrannizing whole peoples of brothers and sisters.
Injustices of societies against societies are not crimes of a Stalin or Mussolini, they are crimes of collectivities. This is also true of the dictatorship in Romania: They were the crimes of a group of criminals."

Content

Foreword 7

Introduction 9

1. Review 16

    1.1 Phase before 1945 16
    1.2 Developments after 1945 21
    Internal party power struggles *23*

2. Armed resistance groups between 1945 and 1962 25

3. Dictatorial violence 26

    3.1 Collectivization of agriculture 26
    3.2 Suppression of the churches 27

4. Repression and terror 29

    4.1 Deportation to the Soviet Union 29
    4.2 Romania's Transformation into a Communist State 30
    4.3 Securitate 32
    4.4 The destruction of political parties 33
    4.5 Arrests and mock trials 34
    4.6 Proceedings against intellectuals 35
    4.7 Arrests of opposition members on the eve of the elections 36
    4.8 The Deportation of Rural Elites 38
    4.9 The German minority 38

5. Relationship between Romania and Hungary 40

6. Withdrawal of Soviet troops in 1958 43

7. Amnesties in 1955, 1964 and 1988 44

8. Cooperation between the communist party and the judiciary. 47

    8.1 Criminal justifications and verdicts of the arrests 47
    8.2 Romanian „Nobody's children" 47

9. Penitentiaries 53
9.1 Sighet   53
9.2 Pitești   55
9.3 Other locations of the penitentiaries............................. 56
9.4 Personal status of the detainees 57
Birthplaces of those imprisoned in percent................................ 57
Penalty of the detainees.. 57
9.5 Deaths in prisons 58
9.6 Two million victims of communist terror................... 59

10. Forced labor 61

11. The Gheorghiu-Dej era 62

12. Danube-Black Sea Canal 65

13. Nicolae Ceaușescu... 66
13.1 Other measures and projects of the Ceaușescu's:..................... 70
13.2 Elena Ceaușescu.. 79
13.3 The children of Elena and Nicolae Ceaușescu........................ 81
13.4 Siblings of Nicolae Ceaușescu 81
13.5 Relatives of Elena Ceaușescu.. 82
13.6 Cult of personality of Nicolae and Elena Ceaușescu 82
13.7 Medals and awards.. 85
13.8 Weapons industry 86
13.9   Prosecutor's accusations and the end of the Ceaușescus 87

14. Pacepa defector 93

15. Iliescu, initiator of the „Front for the National Salvation of Romania 95

16. Departure to democracy 98

5

17. 1965 – 1989 Functional Elites in Romania 99

17.1 Transformation – Development since 1989 102
17.2 Post-Communist Era 1990-1992 103
Opposition parties *104*
17.3 Developments since 1992 to the present day 104
1992-1996 .... *104*
1996-2000 .... *105*
2000-2004 .... *106*
2004-2008 .... *106*
2008-2011 .... *107*
2012-2014 .... *108*
2014-2021 .... *109*
17.4 Herta Müller, German-Romanian Nobel Prize winner 111
17.5 Laura Codruța Kövesi, Prosecutor General in Romania 112
17.6 Elena Udrea, former minister 113
17.7 Gabriela Adameșteanu: The Provisional Love – Novel 114
17.8 Lavinia Braniște: Sonja reports – novel 115
17.9 The silence of a generation 115
17.10 Civil society in Romania 116

18. Review and a possible future development 125

31 Personal reports of some former students of BBU in Cluj-Napoca 133

Bibliography 216

Publications of Prof. Dr. Dr. Johannes Kneifel 221

Foreword

I would like to answer the question of why Romania has moved me so strongly since 1970.
One day my father said to me, „We absolutely must go to Bistriţa to visit my old student friend Michael, with whom I studied at the Faculty of Theology at Leipzig University between 1919 and 1923." We applied in Germany for a 7-day visa to Romania, which was granted. My father had informed Michael that we would arrive at the Bucureşti-Otopeni Airport in Bucureşti on June 6, 1970. When we landed at the airport and went to pick up our suitcases at customs, we were led into a room by two „customs officers". They asked the following questions:
1. who sends you to Romania?
2. do you have contacts with the German minority in Romania?

My father, who was 74 years old at the time, answered the questions truthfully: he wanted to visit his old college friend Michael. We had the feeling that the Securitate officials already knew the reason for our trip. It was a humiliating treatment of „individuals far from education". After a 2-hour interrogation, we were told that we would be interned for the night in a hotel located on the airport grounds. We were not allowed to leave the hotel during the day. The next day we were expelled as „undesirables" on the next flight to Germany. My father was very indignant about this treatment. He said, „The way these communist guys treat us, that's how they treat their own Romanian people. You can see the stupidity and brutality in these communists." We had taken two suitcases of food and clothing for Pastor Michael and his family, but they were not forwarded to them.

35 years later – in 2005 – I flew with Tarom from Munich via Sibiu to Cluj-Napoca. When the plane was over the Carpathians, I „shot" some photos of the landscape from the window. When the stewardess saw

this, she rushed up to me and lectured me: Romanian territory, photography forbidden. She also did not accept my explanation that the satellites had recorded every square meter of this earth. The co-pilot also appeared and explained to me that taking pictures was forbidden and could lead to my arrest after landing. This is how the staff was trained, acting as „enforcers" of the Romanian state power. Such people are incapable of a self-determined life and of weighing decisions.

When I arrived at the airport in Cluj-Napoca, I noticed a big sign in the arrivals hall: Photography prohibited. Now 17 years have passed and some things have changed.

Ceauşescu dictatorship
- Crimes against the own people -
The cruelest dictatorship in Europe after the Second World War.

➢ Approximately 2 million innocent prisoners were arbitrarily held in 100 detention centers.
➢ Approximately 100,000 Romanians were murdered.
➢ Approximately 90,000 Romanian prisoners starved to death or were beaten to death during the construction of the Danube-Black Sea Canal.
➢ 1,165 Romanian protesters were shot by the Romanian army and Securitate after the execution for demanding a democratic and free Romania.

Introduction

In the late 18th century, Great Britain, France, Prussia and Austria became world powers. In the 19th and 20th centuries, the USA, Great Britain, France, Germany and Japan took over this role. In the 21st century, there are only 3 world powers left: USA, China and Russia.

At the Moscow Conference between Great Britain and Russia in October 1945, the zones of influence in Eastern and Southeastern Europe were divided between Russia and Great Britain. The USA had not participated in the conference and did not accept the result. Russia's influence in Romania was set at 90%, by Great Britain at 10%. Russia wanted to exert a greater influence on the country than on other countries of the former Eastern Bloc. Although the Romanian Communist Party had only 400 to 500 members before World War II, the Communists took power in Romania in 1946.

The respected communism researcher Stephane Courtois, editor of the „Communist Black Book" and himself a leftist, describes the crimes: The Communists had killed close to 100 million men, women and children – by neck shot, fusillade or combat gas – hanged, drowned, beaten to death. They were maltreated to death in forced labor or exterminated by deliberately induced famines, epidemics and death marches.

The communists have been in government in Cuba since 1959, in Nicaragua since 1979 and in Venezuela since 1998. There are no fundamental rights in these countries: no free elections, no separation of powers, no independent judiciary. Venezuela had a democratically elected government until 1998. Since 1998, more than 6 million people have fled from the formerly prosperous Venezuela: 5 million to neighboring countries and 1 million to other regions of the world.

Communism has caused untold suffering to people and has not worked anywhere in the world. If communism worked, the Swiss and Scandinavians would have had communist governments long ago.

Romania's communist system developed into the bloodiest system in Europe after World War II. Many of those who had mustered the courage to free Romania from tyranny died in a hail of bullets from the Securitate and the military during the popular uprising. Almost 1200 people were killed only after Ceaușescu's fall. Thus, communism destroyed the destiny of two generations of Romanians. Class struggle and class hatred led to the collapse of the country's elites. As a result, a civil society could not emerge. Ceaușescu ruled the country with state terror. His idiosyncratic foreign policy created distance from the Soviet Union, and his economic policy drove the country into a permanent crisis.

Ceaușescu wanted Romania to become a world power in order to influence world politics. It was an illusion that brought despair and hopelessness to the country. He was constantly on state visits. There were about 200 state visits to all parts of the world between 1967 and 1989. Ceaușescu hated the Hungarians, the Transylvanian Saxons, Banat Swabians, as well as the Jews. With the aura of a red monarch and the state terror of a Stalin, he ruled the country.

Ceaușescu believed he could impress the Romanians and the world with the new government building. Countries like Switzerland, Denmark or Costa Rica would not even think of building a „Palazzo Prozzi". The educated of the world ridiculed Ceaușescu and considered him a fool. One exception: North Korea.

The Romanian Communist Party and its organs are responsible for the crimes inflicted on their own people. 2 million Romanians were arrested during this horrible epoch. 100,000 Romanians were beaten to death or murdered in the 200 prisons and 100 execution sites. No country in Europe left this terrible trail of blood: only Romania.

In all Eastern Bloc countries, after the end of communism, all responsible politicians were put on trial, except in Romania and Bulgaria. There, the communists continued to rule and called themselves „social democrats". They wanted to prevent a reappraisal of the communist past at all costs, since they themselves were heavily involved. In Czechoslovakia, the freedom hero Václav Havel, who was serving a nine-month aggravated prison sentence for hooliganism, was elected president.

In the GDR, leading communists were removed from the leadership levels in all institutions across the board. In Romania, this has not been the case to this day. Especially in the civil service, schools and universities, the communists and Ceaușescu's henchmen are still in leading positions today. Independent research shows that about 25% of the population still mourns the old Ceaușescu system.

Since the political and economic situation in Romania after 1989 did not develop according to the ideas of the educated and active Romanians, a great many people left the country. Many disillusioned and helpless people remained behind.

Many Romanians have left their homeland because they did not want to live in a corrupt country where, in many places, political clans call the shots.

After 1989, about 300,000 Transylvanian Saxons and Banat Swabians and about 40,000 ethnic Hungarians left the country. They had experienced too much, suffered too much during the Ceaușescu dictatorship. They just wanted to leave and build a new future for themselves. They were quickly integrated in Germany, Austria and Hungary because they are very reliable.

If King Mihai I had been able to return to Romania in 1989, developments for Romania would have been different. But this was prevented by Iliescu and Co. When King Mihai I landed in Romania in a small plane from his Swiss exile in 2002, he was banned from entering the country. The same people who had prevented his entry cheered him in 2012 with the words: long live the king.

Emil Constantinescu, President of Romania from 1996 to 2000 stated in an article published in Le Monde on 22.2.1997, i.e. 7 years after the end of the Ceaușescu dictatorship: „It is our ambition to preserve the functionaries and the state companies of the old regime. We want to pursue an independent and anti-Western policy that prevents all changes to our system by European and non-European countries." An opening of Romania to Western Europe was prevented by the Iliescu clique in 1990. In 2004 Romania became a member of NATO and in 2007 a member of the EU, although Romania did not meet the requirements.

Romanian historian Armand Gosu compared Soviet-type communist bureaucrats to those of Romania. In Romania, a similar culture exists: the boss is always right, there is no alternative to what a president or a minister says. The state institutions of power can do no wrong.

Point of view of many Romanians: A Romanian is not allowed to criticize his country, otherwise he will be called a nest-destroyer. Václav Havel, a Czech writer and freedom hero, was arrested three times during the communist dictatorship and spent a total of five years in prison. After the successful, bloodless revolution, he was elected president of the CSSR.

A country has a future only if it accepts not only the bright but also the negative side of its own past and feels responsible for its crimes. In Romania, the Communist Party arrested two million decent Romanians and sentenced them to long prison terms. They were reported to the Securitate by neighbors, relatives and friends. Reason: they wanted to have advantages for themselves. They were completely indifferent to the fate of those arrested. No other country in Europe has incurred so much guilt:
2 million arrested, 100,000 murdered.

After 1989, the Romanian Communist Party under Iliescu tried everything to present the Ceaușescu period in a better light. Iliescu wanted to have the Sighet Memorial closed. It was there that the pre-war elite was tortured and exterminated. Today, the memorial is supported and financed by the Council of Europe. The right-wing and left-wing parties in Romania are still trying to prevent knowledge about the horrors of the Ceaușescu period from being taught in schools. The historical fact, the murder of 250,000 Romanian Jews, is also negated.

The final chapter, Retrospect and a Possible Future Development, discusses the criminal proceedings against Iliescu and Co.

Romania describes itself as a „strategic partner of the United States. In the complex system of checks and balances, foreign policy responsibilities in the U.S. Congress are widely dispersed. Poland, the Baltic states and Hungary have had many friends in the U.S. Congress for decades, and this is reflected in current NATO decisions. The Black Sea is currently geopolitically important to the US. As interests shift to Asia, the Black Sea will not be as important in the future as it is today.

According to opinion polls in Romania, approximately 25-30 % have pro-Communist attitudes and 15-20 % have extreme right-wing attitudes. Both communists and nationalists reject basic democratic values (stable democracy, the rule of law). Democratic structures are therefore very fragile.

As long as Romania does not accept the German-Romanian Nobel Prize for Literature winner Herta Müller as an icon of freedom, Romania will have no future. Chapter 17.4 discusses Herta Müller's courageous and exemplary behavior.

I have tried to chronicle the Ceaușescu dictatorship and developments since 1989, having to refer to secondary literature because I do not speak Romanian.

Babeș-Bolyai University was named after the Romanian physician Victor Babeș and the Hungarian mathematician János Bolyai. It is the former King Ferdinand University, founded in 1581.

It is the only university in Southeastern Europe where lectures are held in Romanian, Hungarian, English, German and French in some faculties. The university has 48,000 students and ranks 1st in the national ranking.

From 2005 to 2017, I held block lectures at the German-language department of the Faculty of Economics of the University of Cluj-Napoca. In addition to the subject of logistics, I also taught political science for a few semesters. Unfortunately, I was told that supposedly there was no interest on the part of the students to learn the basics of political science: democracy, communism and fascism. When studying economics, the subject of economic policy is a foundation for understanding economic relationships.

31 former students of Babeș-Bolyai University in Cluj-Napoca answered the following questions:

1. How did your grandparents (grandma and grandpa) and your parents feel about the years under the Ceaușescu dictatorship?

2. Was the Ceaușescu dictatorship discussed in elementary school, high school and university?

3. How do you and your friends assess Romania's political situation today?

It was a look back for the students into the tragic past of their grandparents and parents during the Ceaușescu dictatorship. They were willing to answer these questions because they were assured anonymity. This shows how deeply rooted fear still is in Romanian society today. According to sociologists, it will take several generations before the majority of Romanians prefer democratic structures to a totalitarian system.

The questions were answered by 17 former students living in Romania and by 14 former students living abroad. I am grateful to the former students for their great support in my research.

They report that sometimes the Ceaușescu period was talked about in the history subject in high school. But this was the case only in some high schools. Most of the time there was a silence. It was also a taboo subject at Babeș-Bolyai University. Only two foreign professors mentioned Romania's tragic time during the Ceaușescu dictatorship and the following decades, which were different in all other former Eastern Bloc countries.

Approximately 100,000 Romanians were beaten to death and murdered in about 200 prisons and 100 execution sites during the Ceaușescu dictatorship. Another 90,000 prisoners died during the construction of the Danube-Black Sea Canal.

Many Romanians do not want to face the responsibility of their history and believe that silence about the most terrible period of their history can heal the wounds.

During the Romanian Revolution, a total of 1,165 innocent Romanian patriots were shot by the Securitate and the army. Of these, 895 followed Ceaușescu's execution.

Thousands were injured. The Romanian patriots demanded a free and democratic Romania. This was prevented by the Securitate.

Since I am now 83 years old, I have certainly made some mistakes, although I have revised the manuscript several times. I therefore ask for your understanding.

1. Review

1.1 Phase before 1945

The principalities of Transylvania, Wallachia and Moldavia were under Ottoman rule at the time of the Second Turkish Siege in 1683 and had to pay tribute to the „high gate" in the form of warlike support. Not all of them complied, as the example of the Wallachian prince Şerban Cantacuzino shows. He officially sided with the Ottomans, but secretly cooperated with the emperor.

As Rusan describes in detail in Chapter 7 of „The Black Book of Communism 2", the Ottoman Empire sought to subjugate Christian Romania.

The Sultan showed no interest in occupying Romania and instead demanded tribute payments. The Romanian Orthodox Church and the Greek Orthodox Church played key roles in Romania's national identity.

On March 28, 1918, Bessarabia and on November 27 Bukovina voted for annexation to Romania. The delegates of Transylvania, the Banat and the Crişana region followed on December 1, 1918. The Romanian territory increased from 137,000 km² to 295,000 km², while the population grew from 8 to 18 million.

Communist Hungary did not want and could not accept the loss of Transylvania and launched an offensive against Romania, which failed. Bla Kun was born in Transylvania under the name of Béla Kun, the son of a notary. He studied at the University of Cluj, where he maintained close contact with socialists. In 1914 he went to Budapest and served in the Austro-Hungarian army during World War I. In 1916 he was taken prisoner in Russia, where he developed into a convinced communist. At the end of 1918 he was back in Budapest. There he edited a communist newspaper. In 1919 he formed a council government of socialists and communists and became the most powerful communist in Hungary.

Béla Kun and his soviet government made territorial claims on Czechoslovakia, Romania and Yugoslavia. The occupation of large parts of the former Hungary by Romanian, Czechoslovak and French troops led former soldiers and officers of the K. and K. armies to fight for the soviet government for patriotic reasons. During the Hungarian-Romanian War, Romanian troops advanced as far as Budapest. This city was occupied for 3 months. This led to the fall of the soviet government. Béla Kun fled first to Austria, later to the Soviet Union, where he worked for the KPSDU. In 1931 he was shot as part of the Stalinist purge.

➢ The Romanian Communist Party was founded on May 9, 1921. From the beginning, it pursued a pro-Soviet, i.e. anti-Romanian, policy and had only about 800 members at the end of World War II.

➢ In 1918, suffrage was introduced in Romania. A major agrarian reform followed in July 1921: over 6 million hectares of arable land were redistributed and the economy experienced an upswing.

➢ Despite a democratic constitution, political turmoil and economic difficulties persisted between 1923 and 1938.

➢ From 1927, the nationalist organization – Legion of St. Michael the Archangel – determined politics. This organization, which from 1930 called itself the Iron Guard, felt connected to Italian fascism.

➢ King Carol II, due to domestic instability, created a royal dictatorship on February 10, 1938: all democratic parties and institutions were abolished. The assassination of the leader Corneliu Zelea Codreanu and other 13 legionaries was ordered by King Carol II.

➢ On August 23, 1939, the German-Soviet Non-Aggression Pact was signed in Moscow.

➢ On June 26, 1940, Stalin demanded that the Romanians relinquish Bessarabia and northern Bukovina. By the so-called „Dictate of Vienna", northern Transylvania had to be ceded to Hungary and southern Dobruja to Bulgaria.

➢ Ion Antonescu was a Romanian general and dictator of the Kingdom of Romania during World War 2 from 1940 to 1944. He led Romania into World War 2 alongside the Axis powers. Between September 1940 and June 1941, he worked closely with the fascist Iron Guard legionary movement.
A. Heinen reports in his book (Romania, the Holocaust and the Logic of Violence) on p. 58, that Antonescu rejected elections because he acted as omniscient and no one dared to contradict him. He believed that he was the „Chosen Savior" of the Romanian people and that only through his ingenuity could he pave the way for Romanians out of difficult circumstances.

The Iron Guard was a fascist movement in Romania. It was characterized by radical anti-Semitism and Romanian ultranationalism. With its 250,000 members, it was at times the third largest fascist movement in Europe, after the PNF fascist party in Italy and the NSDAP in Germany.

➢ Under the authoritarian royal dictatorship of Carol II, the movement was massively suppressed.
➢ Between July 1940 and early September 1940, the Iron Guard participated in government for the first time.
➢ On September 3, 1940, under Horia Sima, it attempted to carry out a coup against Carol II.
➢ On September 4, Carol II appointed General Ion Antonescu as Prime Minister.
➢ On September 6, 1940, Antonescu, with the support of the Iron Guard, forced King Carol II to abdicate the throne and established a fascist dictatorship that brought Romania firmly into line with the Axis powers.

➢ In January 1941, the Iron Guard attempted to coup against Antonescu. After a bloody suppression of the uprising, the Iron Guard was banned.

➢ Antonescu wanted to regain Bessarabia and northern Bukovina, so he joined the fight against the Soviet Union on the German side on June 22, 1941. Within 5 days Bessarabia and Bukovina became part of Romania again.

➢ 250,000 Jews and 25,000 Roma were liquidated by the Romanian army. To the present day, Antonescu's role is relativized by nationalist and fascist groups.

➢ Within a few months, Romania lost 36,000 km² of its territory and over 6 million inhabitants.

➢ King Mihai I had Ion Antonescu arrested on August 23, 1944. Mihai I ended the alliance with Nazi Germany and switched to the side of the Allies. Subsequently, Antonescu was extradited to the USSR and transferred back to Romania in 1946. A court sentenced him to death and had him executed with the most important ministers.

Three coalition governments followed between August 23, 1944 and March 6, 1945. On September 12, 1944, an armistice treaty was signed between Romania and the Soviets in Moscow. An Allied control commission was to supervise the agreements concluded. The Soviets did not care about the Anglo-American diplomats, nor about legitimate Romanian interests. The Soviets forced the Sănătescu and Rădescu governments to follow their instructions.

The Soviet Union occupied Romania and stationed troops throughout the country. According to the agreements reached by Winston Churchill and Josef Stalin and by the Americans, occupied Romania was an integral part of the Soviet sphere of influence from 1945. So-called „patriotic fighting formations" were created, communist ministers and police prefects were appointed just to destabilize the country. They also spread the rumor that the „fascists", as the members of the government of democratic parties were called, were incapable of imposing stable conditions in Romania. To increase the pressure on Romania, the Deputy Foreign Minister of the Soviets, Andrei Januaryevich Vyshinsky, appeared. He was the executioner-prosecutor of the Great Purges in the Soviet Union in the 1930s. In June 1940, he also acted as the „Gauleiter" of the Sovietization of Latvia. Threatening with his fist, he even declared orders to King Mihai I. His two stays in Bucureşti, in November 1944 and February-March 1945, each time led to the change of government.

The states of Central and Southern Europe were expecting the Soviet liberators and not the Soviet oppressors. This turned out to be a momentous mistake, as Rusan reports in his remarks.
Stalin was surprised by the actions of King Mihai I, who had ended the alliance with Germany despite the 680,000 German soldiers in the country. King Mihai I had formed a military regime involving four ministers of the party coalition. The Soviets delayed the signing of the armistice with Romania for twenty days. During this period, they feigned „victorious liberation" by covering several hundred kilometers to Banat and central Transylvania without any resistance. By the time the armistice was signed, the Soviets had captured 160,000 Romanian soldiers. These had originally been waiting to join them. Chaos was deliberately created by the Soviets in order to have a pretext for the Communist seizure of power in Romania.

The Soviet terror against the army, the political parties and the civilian population were foreshadowing the 45 years of terror that Romania had to suffer. It is one of the many tragedies of Romanian history. King Mihai I had brought down a military dictatorship in a coup d'état on August 23, 1944, only to be overthrown by another totalitarian regime within six months.

1.2 Developments after 1945

On March 6, 1945, a predominantly Communist government was formed under Petru Groza. As in all communist states, freedom of the press, assembly and expression was abolished and a unified communist party was installed. Likewise, the monarchy was abolished, and the country was designated a people's democracy.

Measures taken:

- Dissolution of the parties
- Measures against the churches
- Land expropriations
- Nationalization of almost all means of production
- Start of collectivization

On November 19, 1946, elections were held, which the Allies (English and Americans) had demanded. Result: The National Peasant Party and the National Party received 75% of the votes. The result was ignored by Stalin. Instead, he declared the Communists the winners of the elections. King Mihai I was forced to abdicate on December 30, 1947, and Soviet troops ruled the country.

The Red Army remained in Romania until June 1958. It had introduced the state security service and the planned economy.

Opposition parties were banned and all media were placed under the control of the state. Publication was possible only with the approval of the Agitation and Propaganda Department. All activities of journalists, writers and artists were strictly controlled.

Further measures in August 1948

- Teaching was banned at foreign and religious institutions.
- Professors and students who rejected Marxism/Leninism were dismissed.
- New textbooks were printed.

➢ The Russian language and the history of communism became major subjects in schools.

➢ An academy of the Romanian People's Republic was founded. Its members were not intellectuals, but party officials.

➢ Many former members of the Romanian Academy were arrested and interned in the prisons and labor camps.

After Stalin's death in March 1953, the political situation improved. The Kremlin, following the XX Moscow Party Congress and Khrushchev's secret report, tried to persuade the Eastern European governments to de-Stalinize. Just a few months later, Soviet troops marched into Budapest and brutally ended the Hungarians' struggle for freedom. Gheorghiu-Dej asked Khrushchev to withdraw Soviet troops from Romania. This happened in July/August 1958, especially since Romania was the Soviets' most loyal ally. There was little danger that Romania would turn away from the Soviets, despite the very strong anti-Communist feelings of the Romanian population.

After the Soviet troops left Romania, Gheorghiu-Dej lost support. It had become clear to the Communist Politburo what influence the intellectuals in Poland and Hungary had. In Romania, the state's apparatus of blackmail prevented a civil society from forming. Uprisings like those in East Berlin and Warsaw in 1953, in Budapest in 1956, and in Prague in 1968 were unthinkable because of Romanian history. Ceaușescu described Romanians as indolent: „Corn porridge does not explode. Those who live on corn porridge, as Romanians do, are incapable of revolt." Corn porridge is a national dish in Romania.

Already on July 27, 1958, a new wave of repression began with the publication of Decree 318.

➢ Several hundred thousand people were arrested: civil servants, intellectuals, Zionists, homosexuals, priests of various denominations, etc.

➤ Public trials took place in the universities, the ministries and the newspaper editorial offices. The repressive measures ended in the winter of 1961.

At the XXII Party Congress, Nikita Khrushchev had criticized the former Stalin cult and demanded political reforms, which Gheorghiu-Dej rejected. Instead, Gheorghiu-Dej distanced himself from Moscow and sought political and economic support from the West. Several amnesty laws were enacted in 1964, leading to the release of all political prisoners.

In August 1968, Nicolae Ceaușescu refused to participate in the invasion of Czechoslovakia and condemned the Soviet intervention policy. This was positively received by the majority of the Romanian population, and his acceptance grew considerably as a result.

Internal party power struggles

The internal party power struggles were characterized by changes of course and mass arrests. Various groups fought for supremacy.

➤ The agrarian reform of 1948 was reversed and collectivization of agriculture was enforced.

➤ Tens of thousands of peasants who opposed collectivization of their land were arrested.

➤ The Greek Orthodox (Uniate) Church was banned.

➤ On June 11, 1948, all banks and large companies were nationalized.

➤ Romania developed a system of forced labor. Political prisons, as in the Soviet Union, were installed.

An estimated 100,000 political prisoners died in the unsuccessful attempt to build a Danube-Black Sea Canal. There were three Stalinist factions, distinguished more by their personal histories than by deeper programmatic differences:

➢ The emigrants under Ana Pauker and Vasile Luca had spent the 2nd World War in exile in Moscow.

Marcel and Anna Pauker were founding members of the Romanian Communist Party (RKP). Marcel Pauker was executed in 1938 during the Stalinist purges in Moscow. His wife, Ana Pauker, was Romanian foreign minister between 1947 and 1952. She died in București on July 3, 1960.

➢ Those who remained in Romania, among others Gheorghe Gheorghiu-Dej, were called the „Romanian prison group".

➢ The third grouping, was called the Stalinist group. Lucrețiu Pătrășcanu belonged to them. During the Antonescu period, the group members had been hiding in Romania.
Lucrețiu Pătrășcanu was a leading member of the RKP. After disputes with Gheorghe Gheorghiu-Dej, he was arrested and executed.

➢ Antonescu was rehabilitated by Nicolae Ceaușescu 14 years after his death. The veneration of Antonescu and the disparagement of Mihai I is part of the ideology of Romanian right-wing radicals as well as the supporters of the former communist secret police, the Securitate.

With Stalin's backing, Gheorghiu-Dej and the „Romanian prison group" won the power struggle. Pauker was expelled from the party during the political purges, along with 192,000 other party members. Pătrășcanu was executed after a show trial.

On September 4, 1949, King Mihai I entrusted General Ion Antonescu with the formation of a new government.

2. Armed Resistance Groups between 1945 and 1962

Only after Ceaușescu's fall did details become known about the various „partisan groups" that had retreated to the Carpathians between 1945 and 1962 and fiercely resisted the communist dictatorship. As a rule, they consisted of up to 40 members. They were citizens from all social classes: former officers, peasants, students, doctors and workers. In their struggle they were supported by the peasants in the Carpathians, who supplied them with food. Their goal was the liberation of Romania from communist tyranny. The Securitate combed the Carpathians and arrested the resistance fighters, who were brutally tortured and then executed. Romanians did not learn until after 1989 that peasants and deserted soldiers in the Carpathians had waged an armed partisan struggle against the army and the Securitate.

3. Dictatorial violence

3.1 Collectivization of agriculture

The Romanian communists considered the peasants who resisted collectivization as reactionary elements. In the first phase of collectivization of agriculture, starting in 1945, the lands of the Transylvanian Saxons and the Banat Swabians, as well as the Romanian peasants' landholdings of over 50 hectares, were expropriated.

Peasant uprisings occurred in all parts of Romania and were brutally put down. There were arrests and deportations.

On March 5, 1949, the Romanian Workers' Party decided on the socialist conversion of agriculture along the lines of the Soviet collective farms of the 1930s. As Thomas Cuntze reported, the deputy minister of agriculture at the time, Nicolae Ceaușescu, was responsible for the measures.

In July and August 1949, there were dozens of spontaneous local revolts in Bihor, Arad and Botoșani, and in July 1950 in Drăgănești-Vlașca and Vrancea. Troops of the Securitate, the army and the police put down these uprisings. Deaths, arrests and deportations were the result. According to official figures at the time, over 80,000 peasants were arrested between 1949 and 1952.

The independent peasants could only choose between collectivization or being charged with sabotage and thus imprisonment. Collectivization meant not only the loss of the land, but also of the houses, barns and warehouses. They were also deprived of their animals (horses, cows, chickens, etc.) and all agricultural machinery and tools were confiscated. There was no region in Romania where there were not revolts of the peasants against the agricultural collectivization.

On November 30, 1961, Gheorghiu-Dej told a Central Committee meeting that in the fight against the „nouveau riche" peasants, more than 80,000 of them had been tried and convicted in summary proceedings.

In April 1962, Gheorghiu-Dej declared collectivization complete: 96% of arable land was collectivized. As Thomas Cuntze reports, on April 25, 1962, 11,000 collectivized (expropriated) peasants were transported to București in buses to thank the Communist Party for their expropriation. It doesn't get any crueler than that.

The Groza government had passed the agricultural reform:

➢ 50 hectares was the maximum size of a farm.

➢ On April 25, 1962, the complete collectivization of agriculture was announced: 3.2 million peasants lost their land and had to work on collective farms.

3.2 Suppression of the churches

After 1945, the Romanian Orthodox Church was the last major opposition to communist development. In 1948, Romania had a total population of 16 million.

➢ 10.5 million Romanians were members of the Roman Orthodox Church.

➢ Church property was nationalized, and church schools and monasteries were dissolved.

➢ Christmas and Easter celebrations were banned.

➢ More than 2,000 Orthodox clergy ended up in prison or in a labor camp.

➢ After the death of Patriarch Nicodim on February 28, 1948, the Roman Orthodox Church had to subordinate itself to the state. All activities of the churches were placed under the control of the Ministry of the Church.

➢ On June 17, 1948, the Concordat with the Vatican was dissolved. The Catholic Church was not banned, since the majority of the Hungarian minority were Catholics. The Romanian rulers avoided anything that could have been interpreted by Communist Hungary as an action against the Hungarian minority in Romania.

➢ The Greek Uniate Church emerged in Transylvania in 1699, where Orthodox Romanians were converted by the Jesuits. They accepted the supremacy of the pope and were therefore labeled anti-Romanian by the communists. It counted 1.5 million believers and had 1,225 churches.

➢ The Grand Rabbi of the Jewish community Alexandru Safran had to leave Romania in 1948; his successor Moses Rosen was able to carry out his duties until his passing in 1993. The merger of the Romanian and Greek Orthodox churches was enforced by the communist government. Since all Greek Orthodox (Uniate) bishops and many priests opposed the merger, they were arrested by the Securitate and imprisoned for years.

4. REPRESSION AND TERROR

4.1 Deportation to the Soviet Union

Communism is characterized by terror, violence and crime all over the world. Although its development varied from country to country, the oppression and servitude of peoples was an essential element. Class struggle, part of communist ideology, considered the bourgeoisie, big landowners, capitalists and fascists as its enemies. But also the comrades-in-arms and party comrades were often liquidated. Communism used murder as an instrument. Although the Soviet Union was a founding member of the United Nations in 1948 and had ratified the Universal Declaration of Human Rights, it disregarded this agreement in the Soviet Union and satellite states.

From October 1944, thousands of Romanians, Hungarians, Germans and Austrians were forcibly interned as „fascists" in the camps of Târgu Jiu, Caracal, Slobozia. Most of these people had no connection with fascism.

➢ Among the executors of the insane operations was the Romanian version of the SMERSCH, that is, the Romanian Mobile Brigades established by the NKVD (Action for the Arrest and Murder of Germans and German-born Citizens of the Soviet Union by the People's Commissariat for Internal Affairs) in the fall of 1944.

➢ Many of the arrests and assassinations of that period were carried out by members of the National Democratic Front (N.D.F.). The N.D.F. included the Communist Party and other parties and organizations dependent on them.

Herta Müller describes the individual fates in her novel „Atemschaukel", which is based on experiences of the poet Oskar Pastior.
Engineers and technicians of German descent were to rebuild the factories dismantled in Romania in the USSR.

Mrs. Dr. phil. Mariana Gorczyca describes in her publication „On this side and the other side of the tunnel 1945" in an impressive way the life in Sighişoara, a small town in Transylvania. She describes in a historical novel the deportation of the ethnic Germans to Russia. On December 31, 1944, and January 3 and 6, 1945, the USSR presented the Romanian government with a request to „make available" all German men between 17 and 45 and women between 18 and 30. The ethnic Germans were rounded up by the police in collection points at railroad stations. In 1945, about 500,000 Transylvanian Saxons, Banat and Sathmar Swabians were living in Romania. They were loyal Romanian citizens. King Mihai I protested against their deportations in a memorandum to U.S. President Roosevelt.

The Russians had surprised the Americans and the English by the deportations, as there were no agreements for this.

The deportations were carried out by the Soviet occupiers with the help of the Romanian army. Mixed Romanian-Russian patrols went from house to house to arrest those concerned.

About 33,000 Banat Swabians, about 5,000 Sathmar Swabians and about 30,000 Transylvanian Saxons were deported in cattle cars to the Donets Basin to slave in the coal mines 7 days a week.

It is estimated that about 12,000 people of German descent lost their lives. In October 1945, the camps were dissolved and the survivors were transported back to Romania.

4.2 Romania's Transformation into a Communist State

On March 7, 1945, Ana Pauker submitted a three-year plan for transforming Romania into a communist state.

Measures taken:

- ➢ The eradication of traditional political parties through the arrest, murder and kidnapping of their members.

- Creation of the police organization based on a „people's militia" on the model of the NKVD.

- Within the first few months of its installations, the Groza government arranged for several trials of „war criminals."

- On May 19, 1946, numerous journalists were sentenced to long prison terms.

- Further proceedings against former members of the Antonescu government followed in October 1946 and January 1949.

- In addition, the „Mobile Brigade of Romania" made arrests against members of former political parties and military personnel. Charges brought: membership in a fascist organization.

- During the first two months of the Groza government, approximately 90,000 arrests were made.

- In May 1946, General Aurel Aldea, Minister of the Interior in the first Sănătescu cabinet, was arrested. In addition, many members of the tradition-rich National Peasant Party were arrested. They were accused of planning to overthrow the government.

The Soviet Liberator People

Stalin ordered the establishment of National Committees in Moscow in May 1943. Members were to be the Communists who had emigrated to Moscow and were to take over power in the individual satellite states at the end of the war. Foreign espionage was coordinated by the NKVD and the INO.

Another organization of the NKVD took over the prosecution of so-called spies. Communism exported to the countries of Central and Eastern Europe was based on the experience of three decades of terror.

4.3 Securitate

At the age of 28, Emil Bodnăraş was fascinated by communism and emigrated to the USSR in 1932. Experiencing the methods of communism in Moscow, he fled to Western Europe. Upon his return to Romania in 1934, he was arrested and sentenced to ten years in prison. After years of imprisonment, he was released and became a member of the Romanian Communist Party in 1940. He was Romanian Minister of Defense between 1947 and 1955.

The political trials consisted of the implementation of Bolshevik doctrine and practice as carried out in Russia since 1917. Death sentences, long prison terms, and forced departures to Western Europe were the measures taken by the Communists.

A Securitate report of August 27, 1945, listed 10,085 arrests and 3,560 internments. These were measures ostensibly to purge the army and police of opponents of the Soviets. In Romania, the security apparatus, the forerunner of the notorious Securitate, was headed by Emil Bodnăraş.

On August 28, 1948, the Directorate of People's Security was created, also known as Securitate. Its mission was stated in Decree 1512 of August 28, 1948: Defense of the Democratic Achievements and Protection of the Romanian People's Republic against internal and external enemies. In other words: opponents of the communist position of power.

The leaders of the Securitate were appointed by the Soviets and were characterized by brutality. Romania was divided into 10 administrative districts and Russian advisors were in charge of the tasks. The goal was to intimidate the population while preventing any form of personal initiative. Between 1948 and 1964, 2,000,000 Romanians were arrested. Cicerone Ioniţoiu reports that 200,000 prisoners died in prisons. 200 prisons/concentration camps and 93 execution and firing squad sites were located in all parts of the country. Motto of the Securitate: „We torture and exterminate Romanians who are against the communist regime".

The Securitate is said to have had 85,000 full-time employees and approximately 800,000 unofficial informants. The unofficial Securitate employees practiced a bourgeois profession and were present in all areas of society.

The Romanian Securitate border troops were able to shoot at people immediately at the border. They had machine guns, armored cars, tear gas grenades, electrically charged rubber truncheons, and sheepdogs. Overall, the Securitate's budget was unlimited. It was subordinate to the Minister of the Interior, who was a confidant of the dictator. This organization also had tanks and aircraft at its disposal.

The Securitate comprised 6 departments:

1. Control and suppression of dissent.
2. Control of the economy.
3. Cooperation with the army.
4. Counterintelligence at home and control of Romanian citizens' contacts with foreigners. Any Romanian who had contacts with foreigners had to report this.
5. Officially responsible for the protection of foreign diplomats. Later it also became a „bodyguard guard" for the Ceaușescus.
6. Investigative Services.

4.4 The destruction of political parties

Between 1947 and 1948, Romania's democratic elite was destroyed.

➢ On July 14, 1947, at Tămădău Airport southeast of București, leading members of the National Peasant Party were arrested as they attempted to flee by plane to Western Europe. The party was banned for resisting the communist regime.

➢ In October/November 1947, the trial of the leaders of the National Peasant Party was carried out. The leading members of the National Peasant Party, Iuliu Maniu and Ion Mihalache, were sentenced to life imprisonment for „high treason". Iuliu Maniu, Ion Mihalache and Victor Rădulescu-Pogoneanu endured their martyrdom to the end. They died in prison. The same fate befell the leading members of the Liberal and Social Democratic parties in the following years.

➢ On May 15, 1948, several thousand members of the „Brotherhoods of the Cross" were arrested, a nationalist youth organization that had its origins in the nationalist fascist-oriented Iron Guard, which was disbanded in 1941.

➢ At the same time, the economic trials began, involving numerous businessmen for alleged sabotage. In addition, there were phantom trials along Soviet lines: industrialists, members of democratic parties, Freemasons, clergymen, students, former Iron Guard party members, or people accused of alleged ties to Western countries.

They were accused of working against the Romanian communist system.

4.5 Arrests and mock trials

The series of arrests continued in the summer of 1948 and in the months that followed with the arrest of a large number of Greek Catholic priests and bishops. They had resisted the dissolution of their denomination and its incorporation into the Greek Orthodox Church. Roman Catholic clergy were accused of spying for the Vatican and the United States.

More espionage trials against Romanian employees working in foreign representations followed.

- Three hundred pupils and students in Bucureşti were also arrested without reason. They were accused of borrowing books from the French Library in Bucureşti.
- The Trial of High Finance" is another example of Securitate methods. The accused group included big businessmen such as Alexandru Popp, Ioan Bujoiu, Max Auschnitt, Admiral Horia Macellariu, as well as Nicolae Pătraşcu and Nistor Chioreanu. They were sentenced to life imprisonment or 25 years of hard labor.
- In 1949, the Political Bureau of the Communist Party dealt with the returned Romanian prisoners of war interned in camps.
- In 1949, arrests occurred in Banat, where the Yugoslav ethnic group lived.
- In 1952, peasants were released from prisons on a temporary basis as they were required to work in the fields.

Between 1948 and 1952, tens of thousands of schoolchildren, students, workers and peasants who had belonged to anti-communist groups were arrested.

- In 1953, the Politburo deliberated on future „trials" of Zionist spies.
- At the trial of the „40 parachutists", Gheorghiu Dej stated, „This is not about convicting them of multiple offenses. This is solely about shooting them. In the same way, those who had given them refuge must also be shot. 40 paratroopers should be punished differently, but some must be shot."

Tens of thousands of trials were conducted on the orders of the Communist Party. The charges were always „treason", „crimes against the socialist order", and „espionage".

4.6 Proceedings against intellectuals

Degrading trials were staged. Innocent people were confronted with the charge of having spoken negatively about the Romanian Communist Party.

➢ In București, trials were held against the composer Mihail Andricu, the sculptor Milița Petrașcu, and the Marius Nasta family of doctors. In chants, the audience in the court demanded the death penalty for the defendants. The audience were Securitate employees.

➢ In București, famous soloists of the Opera in București: **Șerban Tassian, Valentina Crețoiu, Dinu Bădescu, Cornelia Gavrilescu** – were sentenced to seven years in prison each in a shady trial as „political hooligans".

➢ According to Gabanyi, Ceaușescu and Iliescu were very similar in their statements. Thus, Ceaușescu referred to the revolutionaries as „hooligans", while Iliescu called them „thugs".

➢ In 1960, more trials were held against Romania's leading intellectuals. Constantin Noica and Dinu Pillat, belonged to the intellectual elite of the country.

Thus, as in 1950, any questioning of communism was again to be nipped in the bud.

4.7 Arrests of opposition members on the eve of the elections

In the summer of 1946, there were renewed arrests outside the Pro-Communist Bloc (PKB). The aim was to keep the representatives of the independent National Peasant Party, the National Liberals and the Social Democrats away from the campaign and the elections.
Rusan describes in detail the arrest of the opponents of the communist system. – With the signing of the peace treaty between Romania and the USSR on February 10, 1947, Bessarabia, North Bukovina and South Dobruja fell to the Soviet Union. Northern Transylvania once again became part of Romania. In addition, thousands of people were again

arrested. They too were accused of being fascists or spies of the Anglo-American imperialists. The accusations lacked any basis. They were executed on the basis of a secret order of the Ministry of Interior. Those arrested were taken to the prisons of Gherla, Pitești, Craiova, Miercurea Ciuc and others.

Laws according to which arrests could be made:

➢ Law on the Purge of the State Administration of March 30, 1945. Article 10 established convictions without trial on the basis of lists drawn up by the Ministry of the Interior.

Under this law, hundreds of thousands were interned in concentration camps between 1950-1954.

Two million Romanians are said to have been temporarily interned in Romanian concentration camps during the Ceaușescu period. In Pitești, prisoners were forced to torture each other under supervision. Romania's elite (intellectuals, clergy, politicians, artists, and former prime ministers) were tortured and murdered there.

Other laws that allowed for arrest without a court order:

➢ Council of Ministers Decision of 2/3 January 1952
➢ Council of Ministers Decision No. 104 of August 22, 1952
➢ Presidential Decree of the National Defense Ministry No. 89 of February 17, 1958.
➢ Council of Ministers Decision No. 337 of March 11, 1964

Article 209 of the Criminal Code was most frequently used: „Subversion of social order". It was a law under which anyone could be prosecuted.

Decree No. 62, Article 193/1, of February 1, 1955: prefects, police, administrative and magistrate officials were convicted of „activity against the working class" with sentences of up to 25 years in prison.

Sometimes neighbors or acquaintances were also accused of subversive activity in order to harm inconvenient rivals or neighbors.

4.8 The Deportation of Rural Elites

➢ During the night of March 2 to 3, 1949, the collectivization of agriculture was decided. Within hours, 2,972 peasants with larger land holdings, a total of 7,804 people, were arrested in their homes and relocated to other areas of Romania.

➢ In the night of June 17-18, 1951, 44,000 inhabitants of the border area with Yugoslavia were resettled in the Bărăgan Danube steppe. The area is also called „Romanian Siberia" because of its climate. They were shipped in railroad trains and abandoned in the steppe. They had to live there until 1955 before they were allowed to return to their former villages. In the meantime, their houses and land had been handed over to reliable communists.

The Romanian soldiers in Bessarabia and Moldavia were captured by the Russians and deported to the labor camps of Kazakhstan and Siberia. Between 1944 and 1947, one million Soviet soldiers were stationed in Romania.

The Soviets' actions were also brutal against the German minority, the Transylvanian Saxons and Banat Swabians.

4.9 The German minority

The two main settlement areas of the ethnic Germans are southern Transylvania (Transylvanian Saxons) and the Banat (Danube Swabians). Internment had already occurred in 1944. Until 1989, approximately 400,000 ethnic Germans lived in Romania. It is estimated that 3,000 of them were arrested during the Ceaușescu dictatorship.

➢ The Romanian Land Reform Law of March 23, 1945 was primarily directed against the Romanian Germans until the end of World War 2. They were all considered „collaborators" of the Third Reich.

About 75% of the Romanian Germans lived in rural areas. Of them, 95% were expropriated.

- In 1951 there was a great show trial against the Catholic Church in Banat. The bishop of the Banat diocese, Dr. Augustin Pacha, was sentenced to 18 years in prison. The German-born disciples Eugen Resch-Boncea, Engelhard Mild and Alfred Prack were sentenced to maximum penalties.
- In Banat there was the Weresch-Reb trial, in Transylvania the Schwarz-Kirche trial, and in Sankt-Annensee, Cisnădie, Prejba and Sebes other trials.
- In 1958, the Brașov city pastor Dr. Konrad Möckel, was sentenced to life imprisonment along with eight youths.
- In 1959, a writers' trial took place in Brașov against five German authors: Andrea Birkner, Wolf von Aichelburg, Georg Scherg, Hans Bergel and Harald Siemund.
- In the Northern Transylvanian Trial of the Reen and German Zeppelin Groups, Hans Kirschlager was sentenced to 25 years in prison.
- In 1987, Georg Horn, who was of German origin and came from Satu Mare, was beaten to death by the Securitate in București in front of the German Embassy.
- In 1989, Roland Hirsch, a Swabian from Banat, was murdered by the Securitate.

Romania's communists prevented the emergence of a civil society by making opponents of the regime disappear or beating them to death. This brutality did not exist in any of the Eastern Bloc countries.

5. Relationship between Romania and Hungary

P. Bognar outlined the difficult relationship between Romania and Hungary in an article that appeared in the journal Ost-West-Europäische 4/2004 . The Hungary-Romania relationship can only be understood historically. The history of both nations was for long stretches determined by conflicts, wars and oppression. To this day, their relationship is marked by mistrust. The bone of contention has always been Transylvania. For both Hungary and Romania, this region is considered the „historical cradle" of their nations. A dispute rages between historians and politicians as to which nation was first in Transylvania. Romanian historians have for centuries held the view that the Romanians are the descendants of the Dacians. After being subjugated by the Roman Emperor Traian in 106 AD, they mixed with the Romans and adopted their language. The Hungarian historians deny the Dacian origin of the Romanians. They argue that at the beginning of the 10th century the Magyars, the Avars and the Bulgarians, but not the Romanians, lived on the territory of Transylvania. The Romanians were shepherds and drudges at that time. When the Romanians immigrated to Transylvania is historically disputed. Between the Roman withdrawal from the province of Dacia in 271 AD and the 12th century, there is no mention of the Romanians in the sources. However, it is undisputed that Romanians immigrated between the 13th and 15th centuries. At the end of the 15th century, 400,000 Magyars and Szekler, 200,000 Romanians and 100,000 Transylvanian Saxons lived in Transylvania.

At the beginning of the 18th century, many Romanian immigrants from Wallachia moved to Transylvania. Land was owned by Hungarians and Saxons. The Romanians were poor shepherds and drudges.

The eastern Transylvanian Szeklerland is home to the Hungarian ethnic group with its own customs. While in Szeklerland less than 20% of the population are Romanians, in the region of Cluj-Napoca it is exactly the opposite.

In the 1920 Trianon Peace Treaty, Hungary lost 1/3 of its population and 2/3 of its territory to neighboring states. Romania received Transylvania, the southern part of Maramureș, the area around Körös and the eastern Banat. Approximately 2 million Hungarians lived in these areas. During World War II, Hungary was able to realize its long-cherished plans for revision. In the First and Second Vienna Arbitration Awards, Hungary received back the territories it had lost after the 1920 peace treaty. Northern Transylvania became part of Hungary again in 1940.

Gheorghe Gheorghiu-Dej allowed autonomy in Szeklerland in 1952. In 1968 Ceaușescu abolished autonomy in Szeklerland again and harassed the Hungarian minority. Ceaușescu deliberately neglected Transylvania, fearing that it might one day become part of Hungary again. Romanian historians had explained to Ceaușescu that nothing in the history of a nation is eternal. Poland, too, did not exist as a state for 100 years. It was partitioned in 1772, 1793 and 1795 and became a sovereign nation after the Treaty of Versailles in 1919.

Ceaușescu sent Romanian intelligence agents of Hungarian descent to Hungary to infiltrate the Hungarian freedom movement. Wilhelm Einhorn, vice chief of Romanian foreign espionage was sent to Hungary by Ceaușescu. There he was to lead the operation against Hungary and at the same time inform the Soviet ambassador Yuri Andropov.

Imre Nagy, the betrayed Hungarian prime minister, was taken to Romania with other participants of the Hungarian uprising, tortured there and executed in Bucureşti in 1958.

The waves of arrests and trials:

- For solidarity with the Hungarian popular uprising of 1956, 2,000 students were arrested in Timişoara alone and imprisoned for days in a barrack in Becicherecu Mic. The spokesmen, students of the Technical University, were sentenced to long prison terms.

- In București, students of medicine, law, literature, architecture, philosophy and journalism protested on November 5, 1956. On the same day in Budapest, Soviet tanks crushed the Hungarian uprising.
- In Iași, in April 1957, philosophy students who were preparing a celebration of the 500th anniversary of the accession to the throne of Ștefan the Great, the prince of Moldavia, were arrested.
- In Cluj-Napoca, too, students from various faculties were sentenced to long prison terms.

These draconian measures were still being taken in Romania when a period of détente was already beginning in Poland, Czechoslovakia and even Hungary.

In the basic treaty signed between Romania and Hungary in 1996, the linguistic and cultural rights of the Hungarians were stipulated in addition to the inviolability of the borders. Hungarian and Romanian members of the European Parliament also clash sporadically. It is always about Transylvania. They have been admonished several times by the EU Commission to maintain a factual dialogue. Hungarian nationalists cannot accept that Transylvania is part of Romania. Romanian nationalists demand incorporation of the Republic of Moldova, although only 26% citizens of Moldova want the country to be part of Romania.

The growing interest of Hungarian government politicians in their Transylvanian compatriots is causing irritation among Romanians. In 2013, a dispute over the historic flag of the Szekler escalated into a flag war. Romanian officials had ordered the blue-and-yellow flag with the sun and crescent, the symbols of the Szeklers, removed from public buildings. When the Hungarian government protested against this, it received as a reply that it should not interfere in internal Romanian affairs. Hungary and Romania still have a long and rocky road ahead of them before they can achieve reconciliation.

6. WITHDRAWAL OF SOVIET TROOPS IN 1958

After the withdrawal of Soviet troops from Romania, a new wave of terror followed. Emil Bodnăraş had agreed with the First Secretary of the KPSDU, Nikita Khrushchev, on the withdrawal of Soviet troops.

➢ They should have left Romania after the signing of the peace treaty on February 10, 1947, but they did not. As a pretext, the Soviets gave the need to maintain a corridor to the occupation zone in Austria. By 1955, Soviet troops had withdrawn from Austria but remained in Romania and Hungary.

➢ When the Red Army left Romania in 1958, the Romanian Communists were surprised. They followed Leninist-Stalinist dogmas more closely than the Russian Communists. The Romanian Communists ensured that between 1958 and 1962 there were again arrests of students, pastors and intellectuals. The charges were sabotage, hostile discussions, and „subversion" of the state order.

➢ As can be seen from the Securitate's archive files, the courts had to make their judgments according to the Securitate's instructions.

➢ It is historically unclear whether Ceauşescu brought about the Soviet troop withdrawal in order to implement an independent foreign policy; see: Nicolae Ceauşescu, The Genius of the Carpathians. A give-and-take policy had developed between the USSR and Romania.

➢ The Soviets supported the Romanian Communist Party in eliminating the old democratic parties. In return, the Romanians supported the USSR in its action against Hungary in 1956. In 1958, the Soviets withdrew their troops from Romania.

According to Gabanyi, many army personnel were discharged from service after the withdrawal of Soviet troops in 1958.

7. Amnesties in 1955, 1964 and 1988

During the 45 years of communism there were some amnesties, which were caused by external circumstances but were also a consequence of inner-party struggles for power.

- In 1955, due to the Geneva agreement between Eisenhower and Khrushchev, there was a relaxation of international relations. Numerous prisons in Romania were dissolved and prisoners sentenced to light sentences were released.
- In 1964, the Communist Workers' Party declared its independence from Moscow and sought trade links with the West.
- Western countries demanded the release of political prisoners. Many were released in August 1964.

In the years that followed, there were no longer hundreds of thousands of arrests, but there were still thousands.

- In 1988, a third act of pardon took place on the occasion of the dictator's 70th birthday. Political prisoners released from prison were allowed to leave Romania for the West. It was a measure of the dictatorship to secure tranquility in the country.

Ceaușescu and his accomplices continued to indoctrinate and manipulate the population.

Further protests against the regime nipped in the bud:

- 1977: The public protests of the writer Paul Gomas.
- 1979: The protest of the doctor Ionel Cană.
- Doina Cornea, born May 30, 1929 in Brașov, died May 4, 2018 in Cluj-Napoca, published 31 letters of protest against the Ceaușescu regime between 1982 and 1989, which she illegally transmitted to Radio Free Europe.

In 1983 she was dismissed from Babeş-Bolyai University. She was interrogated by the Securitate, beaten and threatened with death. After the 1989 revolution, she was briefly a member of the Council of the Front for National Salvation.

In 1989 she was appointed the first honorary citizen of Timişoara.

➢ Vasile Paraschiv resigned from the RKP in 1968. He supported Paul Goma, who spoke out for human rights in Romania. As a result, he was arrested by the Securitate and placed in a psychiatric ward. In the following years, he was arrested several times in order to break his will.

In two autobiographical books he describes the methods of the Securitate. In December 2008, the highest Romanian award, the „Star of Romania", was to be presented to him by President Traian Băsescu at Cotroceni Castle. Vasile Paraschiv refused the award, calling the Romanian president an old communist. He died in Ploieşti on February 4, 2011.

➢ Gheorghe Ursu was a statistician and writer. In 1979 he exposed the cynicism of the Ceauşescu dictatorship and paid for it with his life. His son is still fighting today for the clarification of the murder committed in 1985.

➢ Radu Filipescu was born on December 26, 1955 in Târgu Mureş. As a protest against the neo-Stalinist dictatorship in Romania, the young electrical engineer Radu Filipescu printed about 10,000 leaflets in his parents' basement between December 1982 and May 1983 and deposited them in mailboxes in Bucureşti. On May 7, 1983, he was arrested by the Securitate, interrogated and sentenced to 10 years in prison. Filipescu actively participated in the Romanian Revolution of 1989 and was arrested by the Securitate on December 22, 1989. This was three days before the execution of Nicolae and Elena Ceauşescu.

His act of protest can be compared with those of the Scholl siblings at the University of Munich. The siblings Hans and Sophie Scholl were members of the White Rose, who were active in the resistance against National Socialism during World War 2. On February 18, 1943, the siblings were surprised by the janitor while handing out leaflets at Munich University and denounced to the Gestapo. As early as February 22, 1943, they were sentenced to death by the People's Court and beheaded by guillotine in Munich's Stadelheim prison. Their grave is located in the cemetery at Perlacher Forst (grave no. 73-1-18/19).

600 street names, schools and kindergartens were named after them. The forecourt of the main building of Ludwig-Maxi milians University in Munich also bears the name Geschwister-Scholl-Platz.

➢ Starting in 1983, typewriters had to be registered. Possession of photocopiers was strictly forbidden and punishable by penitentiary.

➢ Peasants were relocated to the cities to create the „new man", which led to uprooting.

➢ The control of citizens and the growing number of informal workers changed people.

➢ The shortage of food, the cold apartments and the constant fear of the Securitate wore people down.

Despite the amnesties, every gesture of rebellion was brutally punished.

8. COOPERATION BETWEEN THE COMMUNIST PARTY AND THE JUDICIARY.

The high number of imprisoned workers and peasants at the time of the introduction of communism leads to two conclusions:

➢ The alliance of the working class with the toiling peasants, as claimed by the communists, was a hypocritical solution.

➢ Some scholars claim that communism was not welcomed with „open arms" in Romania.

8.1 Criminal justifications and verdicts of the arrests

Hundreds of thousands of court sentences are still stored in the archives. The severity of the punishments changed periodically.

➢ Before 1948, low sentences were handed down for the most part, i.e. between a few months to 2 years imprisonment.

➢ According to the Criminal Code of 1948, more drastic sentences were passed after 1958. What was still punished with 3-7 years in prison in 1948 could be punished with death after 1958.

➢ The wish of numerous family members for clarification of the fate of their relatives could only be clarified in individual cases. They never learned where and when their relatives were murdered. Some of the files were destroyed or are still not accessible to the public.

8.2 Romanian „Nobody's children"

In the early summer of 1990, ZDF reported for the first time about the Romanian „nobody's children". One could see how the handicapped were vegetating crammed into tiny chambers: unwashed, malnourished, in their own excrement, without any human contact. These images prompted several members of the Bavarian state parliament to submit an urgent motion, which led to the founding of the „Bayerische Kinderhilfe Rumänien e.V.".

The deputies visited orphanages in Arad, Lipova and Şiria. They were presented with a horrible sight. One had the feeling that in these homes „dying would have been more dignified than living". In Şiria there were dormitories with 40 to 50 beds. Urine oozed from the mattresses, making everything more like a cesspool. Gray, dirty and desolate, no laughter on the children's faces. The Bavarian Minister of State Barbara Stamm was deeply affected and personally committed herself to the Children's Aid Romania. Mrs. Stamm was the Bavarian government's representative for Romania.

50 children from Romania were invited to Bavaria thanks to an aid program of the Bavarian Parliament and enjoyed 5 weeks of intensive curative education. Barbara Stamm – Greeting Benefit Concert 1998: „The condition of these children was deplorable. Severe behavioral disorders and a fatal state of health initially called the success of the cure into question. But after only a few weeks, the intensive support, the personal, loving attention of the caregivers and the excellent medical treatment provided by the doctors of the spa home showed visible success. „

In the Romanian facilities, 3-5 children shared a room. The sanitation was indescribable. Often there was no money for meals and medical care was often non-existent. Therefore, the „Bavarian Aid for Romania" was bundled.

Barbara Stamm: „I would never have thought it possible that people in need of help could be crammed in so undignified. Of the more than 100 children we took out of their beds at that time, most could not walk at all, and some of them have incurable orthopedic damage.

Our sympathy, our friendship and our willingness to help will continue to belong to these abandoned children. We want to help them to give back at least something that was cruelly stolen from them: Security, joy of life and a perspective for their future."

Prof. Wolfgang Schramm, who led the Bavarian medical team, explained, „In the years for the „Bavarian Children's Aid for Romania" I have already met more than 10 ministers of health. „
At the end of 1992, Bavaria was the first state to conclude an adoption agreement with Romania. From the beginning, Barbara Stamm's demand was: „Not children for the parents, but parents for the children."

In contrast to Italians, Americans, Israelis, the parents in Bavaria were very carefully selected and in some cases also cared for in the aftermath. Meetings for the exchange of ideas between the parents were organized and the health counseling centers were involved. The children often showed severe cases of hospitalization. In other words, hospitalization is understood to mean all the negative physical and psychological concomitant consequences of deprivation through more or less massive deprivation of social interactions. In the course of time, 100 Romanian „nobody children" were placed in Bavaria.
The center for the disabled in Păstrăveni had a special place in the aid measures for Romania. The Bavarian social services wanted to prove in an exemplary manner that even the most severely handicapped could be supported to the best of their abilities. Older children should not, as before 1989, be allowed to disappear never to be seen again in some psychiatric institution. For the children's home in Păstrăveni, the three churches formed a board of trustees with Romania, the Free State of Bavaria and local authorities.

For the first time, the Catholic, Protestant and Romanian Orthodox churches work together. Since 1990, up to 180 severely and most severely disabled children and young people have been cared for in the home. After their stay at the home, they can stay in Păstrăveni, where they have put down roots. At the continuously created new jobs in the economic sector, weaving, sewing and agriculture, the young people find meaningful employment. The Orthodox Church had to be convinced to cooperate. The patriarch of the Romanian Orthodox Church did not feel responsible for the needs of the Romanian „nobody's children". „We are only there for the spiritual", he expressed.

The projects of the „Bavarian Children's Aid for Romania":

- ➢ Păstrăveni Center for the Disabled – today a pilot project throughout Romania: 180 severely and profoundly disabled children and adolescents.
- ➢ Arad Children's Home – up to 300 children aged up to 3 years live here, many of them HIV positive and infected with hepatitis.
- ➢ Timişoara Children's Hospital – here children with hemophilia and diabetes are provided with vital blood clotting agents and special food.
- ➢ Lipova Children's Home – The 3-15 year old children are cared for in foster homes to enable them to develop better.
- ➢ Rehabilitation center Buziaş „Christian Şerban" – together with the „Christian Serban Foundation" in Timişoara, a rehabilitation center was built where children with diabetes or hemophilia learn to live with their disease.
- ➢ Youth Meeting Center Gărâna – together with the German community, an old forge in the Banat Mountains was transformed into a youth hostel.
- ➢ Children's home Huedin – rehabilitation of accommodation.
- ➢ Psychiatry Brâncovenesc – The buildings were renovated together with Johanniterunfallhilfe.
- ➢ Social pharmacy „Asklepios" in Cluj-Napoca – The project is supported by trainee Romanian pharmacists and doctors in the distribution of donated medicines to the needy.

- Outpatient clinic Râmnicu Vâlcea – A Romanian urologist who returned to his home country from Straubing/Lower Bavaria to set up a medical outpatient clinic receives ongoing financial support.
- Emergency housing area Alba Julia – a project of the nuns of St. Joseph's Congregation Ursberg receives food supplies for the soup kitchen and help for the school.
- „Youth Farm"Ariceștii – in this model for former street children the construction of a group house was financed.
- „German Forum" Sibiu – the activities of the „German Forum": help for the elderly, street children and kindergartens.
- Specialized School for Healing and Care of the Elderly in Sibiu – this institution in cooperation with Diakonie Neudettelsau is of great importance for Romania because there are no skilled workers in the nursing sector (homes for children, the disabled, the elderly).
- „Hilfsverein der Katholiken" București – The association receives medicines that benefit old Russian Germans, i.e. former forced laborers in Russia.
- Alexandria – here the association has donated an X-ray bus.
- Street children project in București – With Caritas of Austria, a house was built for the street children of București. The uprooted children are to be reintroduced into the community, attend school and possibly complete an education.
- Tichilești Leprosy Center – Living conditions in the leprosy center were supported financially and medical care was also provided.
- Children's home Iași – The care of HIV infected children is supported.
- „German Forum" Iași – The activities of the Forum supported both material and medical assistance.

- Barticești Church Hospital – The first church hospital in Romania is supported by regular aid: Establishment of an X-ray department, ongoing donations of medicines.
- Gherăești – A social center with a kindergarten was built.
- Training program for surgeons – Complete surgical sets have enabled Romanian surgeons from Iași, Cluj-Napoca and Timișoara to perform cleft palate and lip tions.

9. PENITENTIARIES

From 1947 to 1989, the Communists arrested over 2 million opponents of the regime, intellectuals and priests, because they could be dangerous to the regime.

In the absence of access to archives, thousands of tape recordings of oral history were made, inventoried, and technically processed. These documents were deposited at the Hoover Institution at Stanford.

The researchers had approached the former prisoners, or their families, through newspaper appeals to help them come to terms with the Ceauşescu dictatorship. Over the course of decades, the recorded data was compared and supplemented. Today, 93,000 fact sheets can be found on criminal personal status, occupation, ethnicity, denomination, reason for arrest and punishments suffered.

The tyranny in the penitentiaries is shown by the methods of the communist injustice system during the 20th century, which brought only unspeakable suffering and death.

9.1 Sighet

Sighet Prison was designated by the government to incarcerate Romania's political elite. Between August 22, 1948 and 1955, about 140 personalities were held in the 72 cells, including 4 former prime ministers and 9 bishops of the Roman Catholic and Greek Uniate churches. 2/3 of the prisoners were over 60 years old, some over 75. Many died in inhumane conditions and their bodies were buried anonymously.
From 1950, the wives and children of celebrities were also arrested and tortured in the penitentiaries.

- ➢ On the night of May 5/6, 1950, 90 democratic representatives of the so-called „bourgeois landlord regime" were arrested in Bucureşti and other places and brought to Sighet in special trains.

They were ministers of all governments from the period 1919 to 1945, most of them were 70, 80 or 90 years old.

➢ Also personalities from the pro-communist government, Petru Groza such as Gheorghe I. Tătărescu as well as his three brothers Bejan, Ventu and Roculet were arrested.

➢ This was followed by groups of Greek Orthodox priests and bishops, who until then had been held in Greek Orthodox monasteries. Roman Catholic clergy were also deported to Sighet.

➢ In August 1951, the leaders of the National Peasant Party, who had been interned in Galați after the 1947 trial, followed.

About 180 people were detained here between 1950 and 1955, 53 of whom died.

➢ Among the Sighet dead were four bishops, several dozen ministers and secretaries of state. Eighty-year-old Iuliu Maniu, leader of the National Peasant Party, and Dinu Brătianu, leader of the National Liberal Party, also died in Sighet. Iuliu Maniu and Dinu Brătianu are considered by historians to be the fathers of Romanian democracy.

➢ Ion Mihalache died after 10 years of imprisonment at the age of eighty with broken health.

➢ The respected diplomat Victor Rădulescu-Pogoneanu, paid for his civil courage with 15 years in prison.

➢ Constantin Bebe Brătianu, secretary general of the Liberal Party, died shortly after his dismissal.

➢ Constantin title Petrescu, died two years after his release from prison.

➢ Many young people died, such as the poet Constant Tonegaru at the age of 33. He was tried for „espionage" for distributing packages sent by the Belgian Catholic Church to poor families.

The exact death figures in Romania could not be done so far, because the 1957 statistics of the Securitate cannot be found and the archives of the operation groups (Dienst-K) are subject to secrecy.

The Sighet Memorial held symposia with the participation of 800 researchers and victims. This resulted in the book series: „Sighet Annals" with 18,500 printed pages of the period 1945-1989.

9.2 Pitești

The University of California at Berkeley has been conducting a research project on Pitești since 2006. „People are afraid of their own history – it's a collective silence", explains the mayor of Pitești, Tudor Pendiuc.
After the country's elite was destroyed in Sighet, it was the turn of the young generation. Started in Suceava prison, the re-education continued in Pitești.

The re-education practices in these prisons were characterized by cruelty. Brutal methods were carried out from December 6, 1949 to August 1952. Method: The victims who were subjected to the worst abuses, brainwashing, had to perform the cruelest torture methods on their fellow prisoners.
After „re-education" they were to be reintegrated into society and no longer pose a threat to the communist regime. The tormentors of that time were never brought to justice, but covered up by Iliescu and Co. There was no country in Europe that incarcerated its own population, two million.

Since 1945, Ana Pauker, Vasile Luca and Teohari Georgescu had led Romania. The successor Gheorghiu-Dej had the prison closed in 1952.
In Pitești alone, 5000 students were detained. In the detention centers of Pitești, Gherla and Târgu Ocna, around 1000 young people were tortured in the process.

9.3 Other locations of the penitentiaries

On the large map in the „Memorial of the Victims of Communism" in Sighet, the detention centers are made visible. In total, there were 240 detention centers during the Romanian dictatorship, including 44 prisons, 61 pre-trial detention centers, 72 forced labor camps, 63 deportation and forced residence centers, and 10 psychiatric institutions for political prisoners.

The same maps list 93 execution and firing squad sites, as well as numerous mass graves.

The political prisoners were imprisoned in the following places:

Jilava   36,1 %
Gherla   20,3 %
Aiud   16,2 %
Poarta Albă12 12.7 %
Other14   14.7 %

➢ The Jilava underground penitentiary near București served as a transit point for prisons inside and outside the Carpathian arc

➢ Prisoners with heavy sentences were incarcerated in the penitentiaries of Gherla and Aiud in Transylvania. Gherla served as a prison for peasants, Aiud for those sentenced to life imprisonment. Both penitentiaries had execution sites.

➢ The prisons in Poarta Albă, Constanţa, Midia, Peninsula, Castelu, Culme, Cernavodă and Bacău were labor camps in the Danube and coastal areas of the Black Sea.

➢ Periprava and Salcia, were the cruelest camps and had a high death rate due to the grueling working conditions.

➢ Baia Sprie, Cavnic, Nistru, Borzeşti and Bicaz were extermination camps where political prisoners worked like slaves.

- Numerous executions took place in the penitentiaries of Brașov, Galați, Râmnicu Sărat, Botoșani, Pitești, Craiova, Zeiden/Codlea and Großwardein/Oradea.
- The women's detention centers were located in Mărgineni, Mislea and Miercurea Ciuc.
- In Târgușor, Mărgineni and Cluj-Napoca the prisons for minors.
- Fortress Făgăraș was the prison for former policemen.
- Sighet was a high-security prison, specializing in the slow extermination of former political elites.

9.4 Personal status of the detainees

Birthplaces of those imprisoned in percent

București	9,8 %
Cluj-Napoca	5,18 %
Timișoara	4,2 %
Iași	4,1 %
Bacău	3,49 %
Hunedoara/Baia Mare	2,74 %
Bârlad	2,3 %
Arad	2,29 %
Bihor	1,4 %

Penalty of the detainees

40% of the sentences were passed without naming the punishment.
1.52 % Duration of liability of 25 years
1.8 % Duration of liability of 20 years
3.71 % Duration of liability of 15 years
4.41 % Duration of liability of 10 years
4.49 % Duration of liability of 6 years
7.32 % Duration of liability of 5 years
7.46 % Duration of 4 years

6.18 %Duration of liability of 2 years
6.64 %Duration of liability of 1 year

9.5 Deaths in prisons

Securitate records show that there were Securitate instructions to conceal the number of deaths in the prisons. In the period from 1945 to 1956, deaths in the prisons were not listed as such. Instead, the place of death was listed as the street, the park, the railroad train, a field or a forest. The cause of death was listed as heart failure, pneumonia, or hypertension.

Between 1945 and 1956, several thousand peasants who had resisted collectivization were murdered. A certain Mihai Patriciu had become known as the „executioner colonel" who carried out demonstration murders. The political prisoners were taken to their village and shot in front of the villagers in the marketplace. Before that, the villagers had been forced to witness the execution. The bodies were left lying around to be seen by the population. Fear and terror were spread in order to break the people's resistance to the system.

Among the thousands murdered in pre-trial detention and at the Danube-Black Sea Canal, some should be pointed out by way of example:

- In 1949, a group of armed resisters was murdered in the Banat Mountains.

- In 1949, 7 prisoners from Timișoara were to be transferred to the Aiud prison. They had to get out of the transport wagon in Pădurea Verde, where they were shot and buried.

- In the spring of 1950, a transport with 38 prisoners left Gherla Prison. They had been sentenced to prison terms ranging from 15 years to life. They were murdered on the transport.

- In March and April 1950, many prisoners were murdered on transports from Gherla, Sibiu, Aiud, Pitești and Mislea prisons to other detention centers.

- Murder of the Greek Orthodox Bishop Vasile Aftenie, the social scientist Anton Golopenia and the two politicians of the German minority Rudolf Brandsch and Hans Otto Roth.
- In 1990, mass graves were found in the forests of Dealul, Măruhui and Dealul Bula-Sului near the town of Neamț.
- In 1991, more than 30 human skeletons were discovered in the yard of the Securitate in Snagov.
- In spring 2000, more mass graves were found in Bistrița.

9.6 Two million victims of communist terror

For years, access to the archives of the military courts has been denied, allegedly because the inventory of court records has not yet been completed.

A study of the collection of court sentences in the „Archive of the Society of Former Political Prisoners in Romania" mentions the figure of 600,000 politically convicted persons.

Two million innocent people suffered under communist oppression in Romania. 100,000 were murdered in prisons and execution sites and 90,000 died in the construction of the Danube-Black Sea Canal. Another 1,165 innocent and unarmed Romanians were shot by the Securitate and the army during protests in January 1990.

Very often, the arrest led to eviction from the apartment and confiscation of property. After release, former prisoners continued to be monitored by the Securitate. Pupils and students were not allowed to continue their studies. Even relatives were forbidden to study the humanities.

Thus, communism destroyed the destiny of two generations of Romania and mutilated the lives of several million young people. „Class hatred", „class struggle", „revolutionary vigilance" led not only to the collapse of the country's elites, but also – thanks to the „dictatorship of the proletariat" – to social murder.

The Western countries and also the USA could not convince Ceaușescu to close the approximately 200 concentration camps that were located in Romania. It was the Soviet Union that demanded and enforced the closure of the concentration camps in Romania. In 1945, it had been the Soviet Union that set up the detention centers in Romania.

10. Forced Labor

Romulus Rusan writes in his Chronology and Geography of Communist Repression in Romania, Vienna 1990, p. 36 et seq. The following:

The „General Directorate of Services" was created in 1951 and dealt with the recruitment and exploitation of young people from „unhealthy social backgrounds","sons of „bourgeois", big farmers, political prisoners, or with relatives in Western countries). By 1960, over 520,000 young people went through hell in inhumane working conditions. Among them were intellectuals like the later composers Pascal Bentoiu and Ștefan Zorzor, whose parents were in prison or had perished.

11. The Gheorghiu-Dej era

Gheorghiu-Dej, a staunch Stalinist, opposed de-Stalinization in the Soviet Union after Stalin's death in 1953. He rejected the plan of the Council for Mutual Economic Assistance (CMEA) to make Romania the „breadbasket" of the Eastern bloc, because he wanted to develop Romanian heavy industry.
Some Romanian concentration camps were closed and the continuation of the Danube-Black Sea Canal project was abandoned.
With the founding of the Moldovan Soviet Republic, historically Romanian land became part of the Soviet Union. Gheorghiu-Dej identified with Stalinism. In 1952, he had the foreign minister Ana Pauker ousted and expelled from the party.
Gheorghiu-Dej wanted to cooperate with all states that did not interfere in Romania's internal affairs.
This led to a close relationship with China. In 1954, Gheorghiu-Dej resigned as secretary general of the party but remained chairman. A secretariat of four members, including Nicolae Ceaușescu, controlled the party for a year before Gheorghiu-Dej again called the shots. Despite cooperation in CMEA, Romania joined the Warsaw Pact in 1955. This meant subordination and integration of the Romanian military into the Soviet military structure.

As Gabanyi writes, Romania was the only Warsaw Pact state not to send military leaders for training at Soviet military colleges from the early 1960s until the end of 1989. Throughout the period, Romania opposed Warsaw Pact maneuvers on its territory and restricted participation in military maneuvers in other countries. In 1956, Soviet Premier Khrushchev denounced Stalin in his secret speech to the XX Party Congress of the KPSDU. Gheorghiu-Dej held some of his closest collaborators (Ana Pauker, Vasile Luca, and Georgescu) responsible for the mistakes the CPR had made so far in Romania. In October 1956, Communist leaders in Poland resisted Soviet military threats to interfere in Polish affairs. During the 1956 Hungarian Revolution, the Hungarian Communist Party dissolved. The 1956 Polish and Hungarian uprisings inspired Romanian students and workers to demonstrate in universities and factories for freedom, better living conditions, and the end of Soviet domination. Gheorghiu-Dej feared that an uprising by the Hungarian minority in Romania could lead to revolution. Therefore, he called for immediate intervention by the Soviets. As a result, the Soviet Union increased its military presence in Romania, especially along the Hungarian border.

The citizens' aspirations for freedom and independence could be crushed in Romania by the Securitate with brutal measures, while the freedom aspirations in Hungary had become uncontrollable. Therefore, in November, Soviet troops invaded Hungary. Romania had granted exile to Hungarian Prime Minister Imre Nagy, but extradited him to Hungary.

With a fabricated trial, he was sentenced to death and executed. After the failed 1956 revolution, Gheorghiu-Dej worked closely with Hungary's new leader, János Kádár. Kádár abandoned Hungarian claims to Transylvania. Romania's government attempted to alleviate discontent in the country by reducing investment in heavy industry and increasing the production of consumer goods. The government declared collectivization of agriculture complete in 1962, by which time 77% of cultivable land was socialist farms (LPGs).

Politburo members Miron Constantinescu and Iosif Chişinevschi criticized the Communist Party's measures in March 1956. Constantinescu advocated Khrushchev-style liberalization. This Gheorghiu-Dej perceived as a threat to his person. As a result, Gheorghiu-Dej removed Constantinescu and Chişinevschi in 1957, denouncing them along with Ana Pauker as Stalinists. Now Gheorghiu-Dej no longer had to fear a serious challenge to his leadership role. Gheorghiu-Dej had the leaders of the Hungarian People's Union party arrested and established an autonomous Hungarian region (Regiunea Autonomă Maghiară) in Szeklerland.

In 2020, there were about 650,000 Romanians of Hungarian origin living in Szeklerland, about 400,000 Romanians as well as members of various minorities such as Roma, Jews, Germans and Armenians.

Gheorghiu-Dej died in 1965 under unclear circumstances while in Moscow for medical treatment. After a power struggle, Nicolae Ceaușescu, who had previously been very reserved, became his successor. Gheorghiu-Dej was a Stalinist while the Soviet Union was in a reformist phase.

12. Danube-Black Sea Canal

The Council of Ministers Decision of January 3, 1950 was adopted on the initiative of the Head of State and Party Gheorghiu-Dej and Ana Pauker. According to it, all persons endangering the People's Democratic Regime and the construction of socialism were to be arrested. As a result, the Securitate drew up lists of „reactionaries", „parasites" and „enemies of the people" who had to toil on the construction sites of the Danube-Black Sea Canal. These prisons were run along Soviet lines. Thus, tens of thousands of political prisoners were to build a canal from the Danube at Cernavodă to the Black Sea. Thousands died. Gheorghiu-Dej ended the project and 23 years later Ceauşescu, with 500,000 workers and soldiers, resumed the project. 300 million cubic meters of earth were excavated and the construction cost was about 5.5 billion DM.

In May 26, 1984, the canal was inaugurated by Ceauşescu. The Danube-Black Sea Canal developed into a large forced labor camp: overcrowding, malnutrition and the most brutal mistreatment led to a controlled liquidation center.

13. Nicolae Ceaușescu

Nicolae Ceaușescu was born on January 26, 1918, to a peasant family in Scornicești. He had 6 brothers and 3 sisters. At the age of 11, Nicolae Ceaușescu moved to Budapest and worked as an apprentice shoemaker. His teacher was a staunch communist who used the young Ceaușescu as a bearer of illegal communist pamphlets.
In 1932 he was arrested for taking part in banned demonstrations. He was arrested in 1936 as „dangerest communist agitator" and sentenced to 2 years in Doftana prison. Ceaușescu was shy and began to stutter when he was excited.
In 1939 he met the very ambitious textile worker Elena Petrescu, whom he married in 1946. She wanted to make a „king" out of the young Ceaușescu.
In 1940 Ceaușescu was arrested and interned in Târgu Jiu prison until 1943. He shared the prison cell with Gheorghiu-Dej, whose protégé he became.
Gheorghiu-Dej, who had been trained in Moscow, recognized the „talents" of the young communist Nicolae Ceaușescu . In 1944-1945, Gheorghe Gheorghiu-Dej was instructed by the Soviets to appoint Ceaușescu general and CC secretary. The function of a CC secretary for organization was always a key position in communist parties.
In 1947 he became Minister of Agriculture, then Deputy Minister of Defense under Gheorghiu-Dej. In 1952 he became a member of the Central Committee after the group around Ana Pauker was „eliminated".
In the CSSR, the so-called „Prague Spring" began and Ceaușescu showed himself at Dubcek's side. On August 21, 1968, Ceaușescu stepped onto the balcony of the Republic Palace and told 100,000 Romanians that every country had a right to its own path to socialism. He was celebrated and these cheers became a drug for him.

Because Romania did not participate in the 1968 invasion of the CSSR, it was courted by the West. Therefore, the U.S. granted the Romanians the most-favored-nation clause in the hope that Romania would distance itself from the Soviet Union. The West granted Romania benefits that no other Eastern bloc country received.

In the 1970s, Ceaușescu pushed a credit-financed industrialization program. Romanian industrial products found buyers only in the Eastern bloc countries and in some African states. Since the industrialization of the USSR, the GDR, the Czech Republic and Poland took place decades before that of Romania, Romania was unable to sell its own industrial products on the world market.

In 1978, the Ceaușescus traveled to the United States for a state visit. The visit to Washington was overshadowed by Romanians living in the United States who demonstrated against the Ceaușescu regime. Nicolae and Elena Ceaușescu demanded that President Jimmy Carter immediately imprison the demonstrators. President Carter tried to explain to the Ceaușescus that people had a right to freedom of demonstration. He explained that people could also demonstrate against him – President Carter. The Ceaușescus were furious and immediately flew back from Washington to București. In București, they were greeted at the airport by 800,000 Romanians who had been transported to the airport in buses by the Romanian Communist Party.

During the oil crisis between 1979 and 1981, the balance of payments deteriorated. In 1982, Romania had to declare its insolvency. Romania was the only country in Europe that had to declare a default. To pay off the debt, imports were restricted. Ceaușescu was granted $13 billion in loans to finance his economic programs. But ultimately, the loans led to a precarious financial situation, as Rau points out on page 13. The social impact was also precarious. Famine and supply problems as well as accompanying impoverishment tendencies among the population were the result. Ceaușescu had demanded devotion and sacrifice from the population.

It is an irony of history: In the summer of 1989, the country's debts were paid off, 6 months before Ceaușescu was shot.

The Romanian Encyclopedia of 1978 refers to the excellent socialist economic system. In 1984, statutes of the RKP referred to it not as the vanguard of the proletariat, but as the life center of the nation. In the same year, numerous purges and extensive reshuffles at the top of the government took place in the party.

In the 1980s, Romania exported agricultural and industrial products to repay the loans. Ceaușescu pushed ahead with an industrialization program: expansion of its own chemical and petrochemical industries, development of its own aircraft construction, passenger car and ship-building industries. In 1986, Ceaușescu purchased aircraft parts from the Fokker aircraft factory in the Netherlands. The machine parts were assembled in Oradea and presented to the public as Romanian aircraft production. The country's resources were completely overwhelmed by the intended industrialization.

The standard of living dropped. Food ration cards were introduced, and electricity and heating were rationed. Between 1980 and 1989 was the most difficult period for hard-pressed Romania. Compared to all the states of the Eastern Bloc, only Romania saw a drastic drop in living standards in the 1980s. This was in sharp contrast to the expectations of the population. The RKP declared that the food supply for the population would be lowered based on scientific and rational findings. It doesn't get more cynical than that.

While the people were starving and lines were forming in front of empty grocery stores, Ceaușescu appeared on television in front of stores full of food and reclaimed the high standard of living thanks to his leadership. The television program reported exclusively on Ceaușescu's achievements. Because the electricity supply was precarious, the television program was shortened to two hours on weekdays.

The way the dictators of China, North Korea, and North Vietnam were cheered by their subjects, Ceaușescu was enthralled. This was to become a model for Romania.

> Ceaușescu was able to literally intoxicate himself with the chants of his party comrades. In parliament, several thousand delegates greeted him rhythmically with the following slogans:

- Ceaușescu și poporul (Ceaușescu and the People)
- Ceaușescu pace (Ceaușescu peace)

Romania maintained diplomatic relations with Israel, although Moscow and all other Eastern Bloc countries had broken off relations. Ceaușescu officially tried to mediate in the conflicts between Israel and the Palestinians. However, he supported the Palestinians in their duplicity.

Only the three communist countries: Romania, China and the former Yugoslavia participated in the 1980 Los Angeles Olympics. They defied Moscow's instructions.

The USSR had recommended that Romania produce agricultural goods not only for its own needs, but also for export. Ceaușescu was enraged by this humiliation and had hundreds of industrial complexes built during his term in office.

The Soviets knew that Ceaușescu was a dogmatic communist and let him have his way. The Western states supported him as he stood up to Moscow.

Soviet reform efforts and the „restructuring" of industry undertaken in the Soviet Union were observed with suspicion in Romania.

Communist companions described Ceaușescu as follows:

> An irrepressible hatred of everyone and everything seemed to be his most striking trait.

➢ He was incapable of admitting his own mistakes and could not lose and was unsteady and restless.

➢ He had internalized the modus operandi of a conspiracy and knew how to eliminate companions.

13.1 Other measures and projects of the Ceaușescu's:

➢ The Danube Delta, with 100 species of fish and 250 species of birds, is considered the densest reed area in the world. The Conducător wanted to use one third of the delta for the production of agricultural goods.

➢ The Ceaușescus had no relation to Old București. The old churches of Alba Postăvari, of Old and New Spirea, the Jewish quarter of Shtetl were demolished in March 1984, as well as hospitals and thousands of houses. 40,000 people whose houses were demolished were resettled in newly built concrete silos on the outskirts of București. Instead, he had the palace „Casa Poporului" built in the heart of București, the second largest building in the world. In his madness, he wanted to impress Romanians and foreign countries. This happened in many cities: New apartment blocks were also built there and the old building fabric was destroyed.

➢ Construction work on the București subway.

➢ In 1965 Ceaușescu caused Romania to be renamed: Socialist Republic of Romania

➢ The dictator planned to destroy half of Romania's villages in order to better supervise people in communal housing. In 1987, there were 13,123, or 20% fewer villages than when he took office in 1965. 90% of the villages consisted of LPG's. The remaining privately farmed 10% produced more food than the 90% LPG'S.

➢ The peasants, after being deprived of their house, garden and field, had to move to one of the 30 large agricultural centers. Thus, Romanian, Hungarian and German villages were destroyed. The systematic destruction of villages in North Korea served him as a model for Romania.

- Since 1980, Romanians have not had enough to eat. Since Romanian industrial products were not competitive in Western Europe, agricultural products had to be exported. Meat was no longer available because it was exported. The ration of gasoline was reduced from 60 liters to 20 liters. Only one 25-watt light bulb was allowed per household.

- Reportedly, most Romanians would not have survived between 1984 and 1989 had it not been for the 10% fields planted for self-sufficiency.

- From 1981, Romanians were told which proteins and minerals were „scientifically" necessary at what age.

- Punishment of 5 months to 5 years imprisonment was imposed on those who bought oil, sugar, flour and other foodstuffs beyond the necessary family needs.

- From 1987, food was rationalized. A daily ration per day: 29 grams of sugar, 7 grams of wheat flour, 23 grams of corn, 27 milliliters of oil, 23 grams of meat, 2 grams of sausage.

- Ceaușescu resumed the program of destroying villages in 1988. It envisaged destroying 6,500 of the remaining 13,123 villages and relocating the inhabitants to agro-industrial centers. Near București, the first centers were still completed in early 1988. The apartments consisted of two rooms and a 4 m² kitchen without plumbing, which had to be shared by at least 6 people because each family was supposed to have at least 4 children. There was no bathroom. In the courtyard was the only toilet of the apartment block. The Securitate officer lived on the first floor. His job was to wake up the residents in the morning, distribute spades, scythes and pitchforks, and drive them to work. In the evening he locked the door behind them.

➢ Those over 60 were often left untreated in hospitals.

Since Ceaușescu wanted to force a population growth from 23 million to 30 million within 12 years, he took the following measures:

➢ Abortions were banned and procreation was declared the patriotic duty of all Romanians.

➢ Those who were childless at age 25 had to pay a childless tax.

➢ Mothers with 5 children received financial benefits.

➢ Mothers with 10 children received a gold medal, a car and free train rides.

➢ A high increase in poverty and childlessness occurred in the late 1960s.

➢ Birth control pills, contraceptives and even expired abortifacients were traded on the black market. Nevertheless, many women, especially distressed ones, tried to abort their unborn child secretly with wires or drugs. As a result of these abortion attempts, as well as poor nutrition, an estimated 11,000 women died. The women who had an abortion could be sentenced to up to 25 years in prison.

➢ The infant mortality rate of 2.69% was the highest in Europe. At the Cighid Children's Home near Oradea, disabled and unwanted children were kept in the most undignified conditions worse than cattle as a result of Ceaușescu Decree No. 770.

➢ Disabled children were born en masse and deported to orphanages. At the age of three, they were examined by a medical commission, which decided on their further fate. After that, the Securitate secret police took their offspring from the orphanages. The chronically ill children, the children with developmental defects due to malnutrition and those who were left behind were deported to homes such as Cighid. There, most of them died of hunger and disease after only a few weeks, or they simply froze to death.

While Gheorghiu-Dej's attitude toward the Hungarian minority was still two-faced, Ceaușescu took an openly repressive approach.

➢ Hungarian-language schools, publishing houses and cultural institutions were largely closed. Ethnic Hungarians were urged to give their children traditional Romanian names.

➢ Jews and Germans fared relatively better: they were useful as „financial bargaining chips" in relation to the German and Israeli governments.

➢ Between 1967 and 1989, the ransom of Romanian Germans by the German government, under the code name „Geheimsache Kanal" („Secret Channel"), was used to obtain the departure of 226,654 Romanian Germans from Romania to the Federal Republic of Germany. The amount of the payments for the so-called bounty is estimated at 2 to 3 billion DM.

➢ Romania and Israel concluded an economic agreement as early as July 1948. This provided for the emigration of 5000 Jews per month. The American Jewish Joint Distribution Committee had to pay the equivalent of 8,000 lei per head. A total of 118,000 Jews left the country for Israel between May 1948 and the end of 1951.

➢ Romania had a fairly effective system of power generation and transmission, but it was inoperable as of 1985. The combined heat and power plants, which also had to burn lignite, were partly operated with black earth. The necessary fuel heat was not achieved. The temperature in residential buildings was 12-14 °C, electricity was cut off in the mornings, evenings and at night, and private homes were only allowed to be heated for 4 hrs a day.

- Corruption was firmly entrenched in all parts of society. Operations and entrance exams to universities had to be „paid for" in kind or with cash.

These measures led to unprecedented poverty among Romanians.

- There was no meat to buy because it was sold abroad for foreign currency.
- There was no marble for tombstones because it was used for the construction of the „Palace of the People".

In the Glasnost and Perestroika period, the suffering of Romanians was considered unacceptable by both the USSR and the Western countries.

Ceaușescu had lost all sense of proportion and connection with his population in the last years of his rule. Warning signals about growing discontent among the workforce – such as the Brașov uprising in 1987 – were ignored by Ceaușescu. He could still rely on the army at this point, although he refused the customary promotion of deserving military officers on August 23, 1989, Romania's national holiday.

The social elite learned English and French in schools. This gave them the opportunity to obtain information from the West. This was one reason why the underground revolt against the dictatorship grew. In 1956, the Hungarian uprising had led to numerous solidarity rallies. Thousands of opponents of the system were arrested.

- Free expression of opinion was punished by penitentiary or labor camp. This was the beginning of the dark Ceaușescu period, which the dictator called the „golden age".
- In 1975, protest rallies of the „Banat Group" took place in Timișoara. The participants were arrested or expelled, s.a. Herta Müller, Richard Wagner and William Totok. Other writers emigrated to France: Dumitru Țepeneag, Bujor Nedelcovici, Jana Orleag.

- There were several attempts to establish a civil society in 1975 and 1976, as in the other countries of Central and Eastern Europe. The opposition members were not able to form parties. Instead, they were harassed, arrested and often sent to psychiatric hospitals.

- The Romanian leadership rejected Gorbachev's catchphrase, which spoke of a „European house." Instead, the Romanian government spoke of a Europe of nations. The Helsinki Accord (Conference on Security and Cooperation in Europe – CSCE –), was ratified by 36 states on August 1, 1978. The document was the result of the policy of détente that began in the 1960s.

- The communist states would not have agreed to any arrangement whereby Romania's internal processes could be determined from abroad. The West, on the other hand, regarded the concessions made by the communist states with regard to respect for human rights as progress.

- Ceaușescu, in a six-hour speech to the party congress, declared that the changes in the other communist states were a „weakness of the governments" and „socialist aberrations." Only the Romanian people remain eternally loyal to communism.

- On August 2, 1977, 10,000 miners in the Jiu Valley of Lupeni went on strike. The workers demanded higher wages and better medical care. Ceaușescu made financial concessions in a personal address to the workers. Afterward, 20 strike leaders were arrested and then shot. Other miners were relocated to other parts of the country and replaced by workers who worked for the Securitate.

- In March 1979, a free Romanian workers' union was formed in București and other cities in Romania. The Securitate arrested members. Numerous writers and artists became symbols of the resistance. Their writings were reproduced and passed on.

- Between 1982 and 1989, Doina Cornea from the Faculty of Philosophy of the University of Cluj-Napoca wrote numerous letters to Nicolae Ceaușescu. She described the economic, social, and cultural policies of the country. Dozens of university professors expressed solidarity with the lecturer.

- Romania was the only COMECON member state to conclude a cooperation agreement with the EU. In February 1988, U.S. Assistant Secretary of State John Whitehead traveled to București to discuss the precarious situation of the Hungarian minority. The New York Times reported on February 15, 1988, that Ceaușescu simply ignored the concerns of the American government. On August 13, 1988, 93 of 100 U.S. Senators voted in favor of a resolution accusing Romania of the „continuing practice of systematically violating numerous international human rights agreements."

- Ceaușescu had Fokker Flugzeugwerke in the Netherlands supply individual parts, which were then bolted together in Oradea. The wings were sprayed with „Romanian Aircraft Company". In March 1989, Ceaușescu told the parliament in București that Romania was already building the most advanced aircraft and could also produce atomic bombs. He was celebrated with cheers....

- He ruled the country with the aura of a red monarch and the state terror of a Stalin. His idiosyncratic foreign policy created distance from the Soviet Union. His economic policy drove the country into a permanent crisis.

- On November 15, 1989, a large workers' rally took place in Brașov. Thousands marched to Brașov and scandalized against Ceaușescu and communism. The leaders were arrested.

- After the events in Poland, Hungary, the GDR and the CSSR, Ceaușescu had scheduled a party congress for November 21, 1989. It was the 110th anniversary of Stalin's birth. He was re-elected party leader again by 3,308 delegates. By 1989, all communist systems had collapsed in all other COMECON countries except Romania.

- Demonstrations against Ceaușescu took place in Iași on September 14, 1989, and in Timișoara on October 16. On December 16, 1989, people in Timișoara again took to the streets to protest against the totalitarian regime. The end of silence: for the first time, the Romanian people showed the courage to stand up to their dictator.

- Der Spiegel of 24.12.1989 reported the following under the headline „A Shroud": „In Timișoara, the center of the predominantly German-Hungarian Banat, unarmed people fought for days in bloody street battles against a highly armed army. „ The massacre claimed the lives of about 1,000 demonstrators. Most died of gunshot or bayonet wounds, doctors report.

- Ceaușescu hermetically sealed the country's borders, cut off telephone traffic and placed Romania under martial law. It was unclear at the time whether, after the fall of the old CP guard in Hungary, the GDR, Bulgaria and the CSSR, the beginning of the end of the dictator Ceaușescu had now come.

- Similar to Leipzig and Prague, the uprising began as a peaceful demonstration. In chants, the demonstrators shouted: „We are hungry, give us bread!" to draw attention to the city's miserable food supply. Students shouted, „Away with Ceaușescu! Get out of here! We want freedom!".

- Demonstrators smashed the windows of bookstores and burned the works of the great Conducător.

- Gunships were used against the angry crowd and machine gunners fired indiscriminately into the crowd. Children, women and men died in a bloodbath. Securitate people rounded up the people and shot them in cold blood.

- While the other rulers in Eastern Europe had long since been deprived of their power, Ceaușescu still resided in his luxurious Spring Palace in București until shortly before Christmas 1989.
- In București on December 21, 100,000 Romanians protested against Ceaușescu, where he was shouted down by the crowd.

On December 21, 1989, Ceaușescu addressed 100,000 selected party members of the RKP in front of the party building in București. Even here, the crowd began shouting him down. The Securitate opened fire, but the military and Defense Minister Vasile Milea refused to give the order to shoot. Since the army no longer followed Ceaușescu's orders, he fled in a helicopter. In București and other Romanian cities, 1,165 unarmed Romanians were killed by the army and Securitate during the freedom rallies, including 895 after Ceaușescu's execution.

The Romanian long-term dictator had sat out the political upheavals in the communist Eastern Bloc – from Poland and Hungary to the fall of the Berlin Wall – and the Velvet Revolution in Czechoslovakia.

At the beginning of 1989, nothing indicated that the country, which had been completely run down by the Securitate and the Communists with an iron grip, would be seized by revolutionary fever. The news of the fall of the regimes in Warsaw, Budapest, Prague and East Berlin had also reached the isolated country of Romania.

On December 22, 1989, Ceaușescu's dictatorship came to an end. Communism had raged in Romania for 45 years. On December 25, 1989, state television announced the execution of the dictatorial couple Elena and Nicolae.

In death, the otherwise inseparable were separated and buried separately in the Ghencea Cemetery in București. Elena's unadorned grave lies to the right of the main passageway, to the left of it the dictator's grave: a cross with his name and a black wrought-iron border.

13.2 Elena Ceaușescu

In the course of the transition from a relatively liberal to an autocratic system pursued after 1986, Ceaușescu had also promoted the rise of his wife Elena.

- ➤ Elena was called a „doctor of chemistry" even though she had only attended 4 years of elementary school.
- ➤ In 1985 she was appointed president of the Supreme Council for Science and Education. The members of the Romanian Academy of Sciences appointed the illiterate Elena as President of the Academy in order to gain advantages in the „Ceaușescu system". The professors of the Academy had neither decency nor conscience to appoint the unqualified Elena Ceaușescu as president.
- ➤ In 1989, she became chairman of the Central Commission for Organization and Modernization.

Elena Ceaușescu told U.S. President Carter during a state visit to the United States in 1976 that Romania wanted to bring Romanian culture closer to Americans and planned to establish 182 cultural institutes in the United States alone.

In 2022, Romania will have 18 cultural institutes worldwide, including in Tokyo and New York. Switzerland and the Scandinavian countries do not need to convince the world of their culture and do not have to maintain cultural institutes worldwide.

In her book „System Change in Romania", A. U. Gabanyi describes the person Elena Ceaușescu as follows:

She was vain, ignorant and also obsessed with titles and awards. She called herself an academic, a doctor, an engineer. The Romanian Foreign Service made sure that Elena was showered with diplomas from the universities of Yucatan, Beirut, Manila, Bahia Blanca and Caracas. In addition, books written with her name, but not by her, also had to be translated into different languages.

Before the state visits to Argentina, China, India, the USA and Jordan, etc., Elena had the Romanian secret service prepare personal dossiers on the wives of the statesmen.

The federal government was in a big dilemma: they wanted to facilitate the life of Romanians and that of the German and Hungarian minorities. Therefore, they gave the Conducător a Mercedes 600 and Elena a Mercedes 450.

Loki Schmidt writes the following in her book „On the Red Carpet and Firmly on Earth."

„Trips to the Eastern Bloc went a bit strangely. So they had some difficulties with Elena Ceaușescu, [...] who was considered narrow-minded and brutal.
We had difficulties not only with the woman, but also with the man. We were received by the two of them in a small room of a palace in București. From there, a corridor led to a large hall. And what would they have done if someone opened the door to the hall and asked them to leave with a hand gesture. Then they would have gone first as guests." [...] So there was the hallway, and Helmut and I went ahead. Suddenly I received a strong push to my elbow and so did Helmut. The two of them pushed us back because they wanted to get into the hall first. It was full of people, and when the dictator and his wife came through the door, cheers erupted. Now, that was pure Byzantinism, nauseating. But such ribbing, as from the Ceaușescus, we have never had to experience again, anywhere."

According to Mrs. Schmidt's account, it was an unpleasant state visit. She looked more brutal than Nicolae and she remembered her as an unpleasant person.

The Ceaușescus' methods became known through the former head of the Romanian Foreign Intelligence Service (DIE), Mihai Pacepa. The latter had defected to the Americans during a stay in Germany, in July 1978.

13.3 The children of Elena and Nicolae Ceaușescu

- Son Nicu was built up as a functionary and successor. From 1983 he was First Secretary of the Communist Youth League, and from October 1989 First Party Secretary of Sibiu County. During the demonstrations against Ceaușescu in December 1989, he ordered the Securitate to shoot at the unarmed demonstrators.

- The daughter Zoia was sponsored by the Deputy Minister of Education Mircea Malița. She studied mathematics. In the 1980s, she became director of the Romanian Academy of Sciences in București.

- The eldest son Valentin is a Romanian physicist who, unlike his siblings, was not politically active.

Since Gorbachev took office in 1985, the Romanian leadership has been subjected to growing Soviet pressure. In May 1987, during a visit to București, Gorbachev criticized family patronage, corruption, the lack of democracy and the alienation between party leadership and the population. By the end of the 1980s, the threshold of suffering had been crossed. Farmers were forced to deliver their products to the state at low prices under a quota system and a compulsory levy. This led to local protests.

13.4 Siblings of Nicolae Ceaușescu

- The sister Nicolina married Manea Mănescu, the long-time prime minister.

- The sister Maria married the politician Ilie Verdeț.

- Sister Eleona worked in Oltenia as a school inspector and is said to have been a district bully.

- The brother Marin became a trade councillor in Vienna. He is said to have set up a spy network in Western Europe. He was found dead on December 28, 1989. Whether by murder or suicide could not be clearly established.

- Brother Ion worked in agriculture and became deputy minister of agriculture from 1972.
- The brother, Ilie, had been a major general and Romania's top political commissar since 1975 and also became deputy defense minister in 1983. He tried to put down the Romanians' struggle for freedom in Sibiu after his brother's death.
- The brother Nicolae Andruță Ceaușescu allegedly shot several demonstrators in București. On July 13, 1990, murder charges against him were dropped for lack of evidence. He was sentenced to 15 years in prison for other offenses on July 31, 1990.
- Brother Florea was editor of the communist newspaper Scânteia.

13.5 Relatives of Elena Ceaușescu

- The brother Gheorghe Petrescu was Romanian head of delegation at the „Council for Mutual Economic Assistance" (CMEA) in Moscow. His wife Raschela „earned" millions of dollars in car sales.
- One of Elena's sisters was married to the minister Cornel Burtică.

13.6 Cult of personality of Nicolae and Elena Ceaușescu

Many Romanians closely monitored the daily press: „Think, plan, act according to Comrade Nicolae Ceaușescu's instructions."

This cult of personality developed with the rise of Elena. She encouraged him in his delusion of being a titan. As reported by Der Spiegel on Nov. 30, 1986, she told him, „You are too big for such a small country."

Ceaușescu built a Stalinist dictatorship with a strong personality cult. Thus, he had himself called Conducător (leader). This title had already been used by the fascist military dictator Ion Antonescu. He also let himself be called „the chosen one, our earthly god or genius of the Carpathians." The personality cult is far more bizarre than the idolatry ever paid to Hitler, Stalin or Mao.

Păunescu wrote during the lifetime of the Ceaușescus: „I dare not mention their names. For fear of belittling their greatness when I speak of them. But history demands it of me. We should all love them: they who embody victory in battle for the people."

Writers praised him as a „titan among titans", comparing his actions to those of Julius Caesar, Alexander the Great, Pericles, Napoleon or Cromwell.

The poets described Ceaușescu as follows:

Ceaușescu
-Our Earthly God
-Grand as the Carpathians
    -You are forever our shining and watchful conscience
    -The new creator of Romania
-Supreme embodiment of good
-A man like a fir tree
-Guarantor of the wealth of Romania
-He is the honey of this world
-He is the legislator
-Without the miracle of Ceaușescu, no miracle of Romania
    -You are always our pride
    -Savior of the world devastated by war
-Source of the living water
    -Titan of our earth
    -His immortality is our burning desire, so he will live as long as our world.

- Alexandra, Ceaușescu's mother, gave birth to a son to free the world from misery.
- Other peoples had Julius Caesar, Alexander, Pericles, Cromwell, Napoleon, Peter the Great and Lincoln. We Romanians had Mihai the Brave, Cantemir and now we have Ceaușescu.

Many court poets of the Ceaușescus changed their praises in a flash after the couple was shot.

Malte Olschewski reports in detail about the characteristics of Nicolae Ceaușescu in his work „The Conducător – Phenomenon of Power":

- Its Stalinist controls in all aspects of religious, scientific, commercial, social, and civil life exacerbated the situation of Romanians.

- Ceaușescu constantly changed party officials and ministers in order to hold them responsible for abuses. During the 25 years of his dictatorship, he appointed and dismissed between 300-400 ministers. The exceptions were his family members, whom he appointed as overseers in all key positions.

- In 1987, a demonstration in Brașov was put down. The army occupied the factories and slew the demonstrators.

- In 1989 Ceaușescu became more and more isolated in the communist world. In August 1989, he called for a meeting with all Warsaw Pact countries and the Chinese to show the steadfastness of Romanian communism to the world.

- After the fall of the Berlin Wall and after the fall of the Bulgarian dictator Todor Zhivkov in November 1989, Ceaușescu ignored the „signs of the times" and became the last Stalinist leader in Eastern Europe.

The birthplace „Scornicești" of Nicolae Ceaușescu was supposedly a place with historical significance. The name Ceaușescu derives from a Turkish Tatar name. When the leaders of the Romanian Gypsy clans had problems with the local party authorities, they allegedly scandalized, „E de al nostru!" – He is one of us! – They meant the Conducător.

Just as the birthplace of Nicolae Ceaușescu was declared a historical site, Elena's birthplace became a „landmark". As the Tribuna Românească newspaper reported in May 1987, Petrești is said to have been a crossroads between Europe and Asia as early as the Stone Age.

Archaeologists reportedly found remains of the oldest hominids (chimpanzees, gorillas and orangutans) there. The birthplace was converted into a memorial and the village street was transformed into a four-lane „Boulevard of Peace".

13.7 Medals and awards

- Although his salary was set at $3,000 a month, the Ceaușescus led a luxurious lifestyle. They lived in București in a luxurious villa and in the country they had a total of about 80 villas and hunting lodges at their disposal.

- About 90 publications about Ceaușescu appeared in 32 countries. A 5-volume complete edition of his works was published in India. The total number of state visits during his 25-year term is estimated at 150.

- In all Romanian embassies around the world, a bedroom was set aside for the Ceaușescus. After his execution, people were surprised at the Ceaușescus' many riches: rooms full of suits and uniforms that had never been worn, gifts from all over the world.

- Foreign kings and heads of state showered Ceaușescu with medals to alleviate the suffering of Romanians. He was pathologically interested in doctoral hats and foreign medals. He was awarded a total of 30 doctorates.

- France awarded him the Legion of Honor.

- Queen Elizabeth awarded Ceaușescu the Order GCB (Grand Cross of the Bath, the Order of the Bath, GCB Order of St. Michael and St. George, GCMG Royal Victorian Order, GCVO). A special feature is the highest class of orders in the two British orders of chivalry that related to the then British India, namely the Order of the Indian Empire (GCIE) and the Order of the Star of India (GCSI). The British orders were revoked from Ceaușescu.
- In 1988, Ceaușescu received the Karl Marx Order of the GDR for rejecting Gorbachev's reforms.
- After his execution, he was posthumously deprived of the insignia of the order. Queen Elizabeth II renounced the high order that Ceaușescu had presented to her and returned it to Romania.
- Emperor Bokassa of the Central African Republic also awarded Ceaușescu a doctorate from Bangui University. Bokassa desired a white woman for his harem. In gratitude, Ceaușescu arranged for a certain Gabriela from the București Ballet to become one of the „emperor's" wives. After spending a few months in Bangui, Central Africa, she managed to escape to Paris.

13.8 Weapons industry

In the mid-1980s, Romania maintained trade missions in 110 countries, including countries such as Burundi, Costa Rica, Benin and Guyana. No trade was conducted with these countries. The trade missions were branches of Romania's foreign intelligence service.

From 1985, the Romanian arms industry was manufactured under licenses from the Soviets. Exports were made, in particular, to Africa. These were tanks, missiles and rifles. Thus, Romania was able to earn 2-3 billion DM annually in foreign currency.
The shipyards built destroyers and warships. On April 14, 1985, the dictator told the Romanian Central Committee: „Romanian scientists

are capable of producing nuclear weapons, they have the know-how. But we do not want that."

13.9 Prosecutor's accusations and the end of the Ceauşescus

Pastor Laszlo Tökes denounced in letters to Ceauşescu and in cries for help to the West the most serious violations of human rights, as well as the planned destruction of villages and the persecution of the Hungarian minority. The Romanian government wanted to depose the pastor Laszlo Tökes.

In November 1989, four masked men tried to kill the pastor in his apartment. For their own safety, the Tökes family moved into the sacristy of the church. When Pastor Tökes complained to his superior, Laszlo Papp, he dismissed him and punitively transferred him to a Transylvanian village. Since the Hungarian minority and the Romanian students rejected his transfer, mass demonstrations broke out.

Despite these escalations, Ceauşescu left for a state visit to Iran on December 17, 1989, leaving decisions against the demonstrations to his wife and staff. With many demonstrators arrested by the Securitate, unrest spread to Timişoara on December 18. The army, police, and Securitate opened fire on the protesters, killing about 100 people. This information from Radio Free Europe, BBC and Deutsche Welle, triggered a wave of indignation in the country. In Sibiu and Bucureşti, the army refused to shoot the protesters.

On December 20, Ceauşescu called the demonstration in Timişoara on Romanian television an agitation by the West to interfere in internal Romanian affairs. Ceauşescu responded to the demonstrations with further, merciless repression. These demonstrations were not mentioned in the media. Romanians learned about them in the Voice of America and on Radio Free Europe. The way the revolution took place, Gabanyi calls it radio and telerevolution, was without precedent in history. Arrested members of the Ceauşescu clan and also the trial of the Ceaușescus were shown on television. It was an uprising against communism and against the communists.

On December 21, Ceaușescu wanted to speak to his supporters in downtown București. Instead, he was shouted down. Unable to calm the crowds, Ceaușescu and his wife retreated until the next day. The following day, people poured into the city center and were met by police, the army, and the Securitate. Hundreds of protesters were arrested indiscriminately. As became known after 1989, the whole of București was crisscrossed by a tunnel system for the Securitate.

On the morning of December 22, the uprising was unstoppable in other cities of the country as well. The unexplained death of Vasile Milea, the defense minister, was announced by the media. Was it an ordered suicide or a cold-blooded killing by the Securitate? Other sources claim that Milea was shot because he did not want to participate in the Coup d'état. Now Ceaușescu also took over as defense minister and tried to calm the masses from the balcony of the Communist Party building on December 22, 1989. Ceaușescu and the RKP could no longer meet the political and material expectations of the Romanians. The latter began to storm the party building.

In order not to have to fly in a helicopter with the Ceaușescus in București, General Stănculescu stuck a false plaster bandage on his leg to feign an injury. In doing so, he changed sides, having previously come to terms with Iliescu.

The dictator couple fled in a helicopter with Emil Bobu, Manea Mănescu and some bodyguards. On the army's orders, the Ceaușescus were dropped off in a field near Târgoviște, as the army had banned air travel throughout Romania. At first, Ceaușescu and his wife were detained by the police and then transferred to the army. His closest associate, General Stănculescu, ensured that the Ceaușescus were arrested by army personnel.

Civil war-like clashes between the army and the Securitate occurred in some cities on December 23-24, 1989. Units of the Securitate had attempted to free Ceaușescu.

Ion Iliescu, a „political foster son" of Ceaușescu and his comrades-in-arms, was keen to see fighting break out between the demonstrators and the Securitate. Iliescu installed his power during these days, appearing in public for the first time when Ceaușescu had already been shot. He justified the Front for the National Salvation of Romania with the fact that Romania had to be saved from foreign agitators who were supposedly already in the country.

Milo Rau in his book „The Last Days of the Ceaușescus" describes how he perceived the trial of the Ceaușescus on December 26, 1989: „two old people [sat] at a table, [...] abandoned by their people and betrayed by their own comrades [...]".

When Stănculescu showed up for the trial, Ceaușescu was delighted to see his close confidant. Only during the trial did Ceaușescu realize that he had been lured into a trap by Stănculescu. Before Stănculescu defected to Iliescu, he had several dozen demonstrators shot during the demonstration in București. After 1989, Stănculescu was sentenced to 15 years in prison and taken to Jilava, the notorious prison outside București. His wife committed suicide. In the same prison, Hitler collaborator Antonescu was executed.

Nicolae Ceaușescu was charged with genocide. The judges and prosecutors accused him and his clique of a lavish lifestyle while the people starved and he had villages destroyed. The people were quartered in gray houses so that they could be better controlled. Ceaușescu declared during the trial that the case against him was illegal and that only the „Great People's Assembly" could depose him.

Ceaușescu was asked by the prosecutor whether he was mentally ill. If he had answered in the affirmative, he might have been institutionalized. Instead, Ceaușescu became angry and threatened, saying, „Just wait and see what I do to you when this is over." The question was raised by the prosecutor whether the dictator and his wife were not mentally ill (just like Hitler, Pol Pot, Kim II Sung, etc...). This was rejected by the Ceaușescus.

Nicolae and Elena Ceaușescu were sentenced to death by a military court after a 90-minute trial. The grand old man of the Socialist Party was to have the mask torn from his eternally smiling face. „He had badly dyed hair. His faulty Romanian, his pathetic gesticulating, his petty-bourgeois thinking were clearly evident at the trial. Elena lost her composure".

During the trial, Ceaușescu repeatedly stated that Romanians would be worse off after his demise.

The military court was contacted by telephone three times during the trial: The Ceaușescus should be shot immediately. Iliescu feared that Ceaușescu would incriminate him during due process. Therefore, he and his comrades-in-arms pleaded for the immediate execution of the Ceaușescus. They held the Ceaușescus responsible for the wretched state of the country. Securitate members had supported Ceaușescu to the end, as they wanted to secure their standard of living while the Romanian army dithered. Iliescu claimed that foreigners wanted to destabilize Romania and therefore founded the „Front for the National Salvation of Romania." He intended to continue the old system without Ceaușescu.

As Gabanyi reports, it became known only years later that the Iliescu group had made all the important decisions between December 22 and 27, 1989.

Before they were shot, Ceaușescu sang the Internationale and predicted that history would honor him accordingly. His wife, on the other hand, shouted that she was the mother of all Romanians and that she wished hell on all bystanders. The court trial and also the execution were filmed and immediately delivered to Western television stations. The trial and

also the corpses were shown to the stunned Romanian public, but not the execution.
The Romanian army cited the threat of civil war as the reason for the execution.

The Romanian Writers' Union had incessantly asked writers to write praises of the Conducător. Writers such as Ana Blandiana, Paul Gama, Herta Müller and Mircea Dinescu never wrote a positive line about Ceaușescu.
After the execution of the Ceaușescus, Păunescu poetized, „Look at him, that inhuman face, with his jaw the size of old stone, that illiterate, that lisping snake."

The graves of the Ceaușescus are located in the Ghencea cemetery in București. They are not next to each other, but are separated by a path. Ceaușescu's grave is still very much cared for by his followers. The Ceaușescus' children tried to bury their parents in a mausoleum, which was forbidden by the government.

After the death of the dictator couple, Ion Iliescu took over the presidency of the newly founded „Front for the National Salvation of Romania". The latter took over the duties of government.
Among the 39 members were scientists (Doina Cornea, Silviu Brucan), clergymen (Laszlo Tökes), lawyers (Dumitru Mazilu) and the writers (Ana Blandiana, Mircea Dinescu, Dan Deslin). They played a decisive role in the final phase of the Ceaușescu dictatorship.
The actual circumstances of the revolution have not yet been fully clarified. The victims were eliminated, the investigation was delayed and the files were partially destroyed.
The spontaneous revolution became an „unfinished" one, a „stolen" one, a „betrayed" one, finally a coup and a coup d'état.
Olschewski argues that the West was partly to blame for the suffering of the Romanians. However, one must also consider the following: the West did not want to risk a war with the USSR.

Doina Cornea wrote numerous letters to Ceaușescu between 1980 and 1989, pointing out the devastating economic situation of Romanians. As a result, she was dismissed by the rector of Babeș-Bolyai University in Cluj-Napoca. When the rector reported her dismissal to the college of professors, the lecturers/professors broke out in jubilation, scandalizing: „giant of the modern age", „light that defies even the sun", „genius of the epoch", „first thinker of this earth."

As Doina Cornea reported, after 1989 her former communist-opportunist colleagues changed sides of the street in Cluj-Napoca when they met her. Professor Doina Cornea showed character and dignity. She was not a shameless opportunist.

14. Pacepa defector

Pacepa had studied industrial chemistry and was recruited by the Secret Service in the early 1950s.
At the age of 35, he was already deputy head of the Romanian Foreign Intelligence Service (DIE) and coordinated external operations. In the early 1970s, he became Ceaușescu's personal security advisor.
Mission: to spy on, blackmail, imprison or liquidate Romanians who tried to flee.
In July 1978, he was on an official trip to Bonn to deliver a message from Ceaușescu to former Chancellor Helmut Schmidt. He did not deliver a message, but asked for political asylum at the U.S. Embassy. The Americans flew him out to Washington on July 28, 1978, because he had extensive insider knowledge about Ceaușescu.
He knew the mechanisms of the Romanian secret service and the interconnections with the Soviet KGB.

As Pacepa reports in his book „Red Horizons", he informed the Americans about Romania's cooperation with Arab terrorist organizations, drug lords, as well as the activities of Romanian economic espionage.
He also reported on forged documents given to foreign journalists and financial payments to journalists who reported positively about Romania and Ceaușescu. He described Ceaușescu as a „paranoid dictator who oppresses his people but lives in luxury himself."

After Pacepa's escape, Ceaușescu purged his staff, as he no longer trusted anyone except his own family members. Securitate generals were arrested or dismissed, especially former associates of Pacepa.
In Romania, he was considered an enemy of the people, a traitor. According to the present-day Securitate Files Processing Authority (CNSAS), Ceaușescu demanded that the traitor be returned to Romania immediately. In September 1978, he was sentenced to death in a secret trial. Although a $2 million bounty had been placed on his head, con-

tract killers were unable to find him. He is said to have undergone cosmetic surgery several times to change his appearance.

Pacepa is controversial in Romania. Historians accuse him of having served the secret service himself. Journalist André de Hilleriu wrote in the Romanian daily Libertatea in February 2021: „You can't just make heroes out of executioners and idols out of traitors." In 1999, the death sentence against Pacepa was overturned by the Romanian Supreme Court.

After Ceaușescu's death, Pacepa demanded the return of his property in Romania as well as the annulment of the verdict and the restoration of his former military position as a 2-star general. President Iliescu was opposed to the annulment of the sentence. Nevertheless, Romania's highest court upheld Pacepa's claim (Decision No. 41/1999). It is unknown whether Pacepa ever visited Romania again. He died in the United States at the age of 92. He was the highest-ranking defector from the Eastern Bloc to the West during the Cold War.

15. Iliescu, initiator of the „Front for the National Salvation of Romania

> Iliescu studied at the Moscow Institute of Energetics between 1950 and 1953, where he served as leader of the Group of Romanian Students in the Soviet Union.

> Iliescu was chairman of the Communist Youth League between 1957 and 1971 and CC secretary for ideology and propaganda between February and July 1971. He was then secretary of the county party committee for ideology and propaganda in Timișoara, and between 1974 and 1979 Iliescu was county party secretary in Iași. In 1979 and 1984 Iliescu was head of the National Waterworks and from 1985 until the fall of communism he was director of a technical publishing house at the Press House in București.

Silviu Brucan was Romania's ambassador to the United States and the UN between 1956 and 1962. Along with Iliescu, he is considered the most important player in the overthrow of Ceaușescu .
Brucan considered Gorbachev to be the engine of the transformation of the communist system. In March 1989, Brucan and five other old communists wrote a so-called „Letter of the Six" to Ceaușescu. In it, he urged him to change his political course.

Since October 2, 1989, a newly founded Social Democratic Party had been working underground in Romania. This party called for „liberation from the chains of communist dictatorships. It called for pluralistic democracy, a free market economy and respect for human rights. The following day in East Berlin, all the parties and groups gathered at the so-called „Round Table" issued a statement declaring: „We stand in solidarity with the Romanian people and their struggle for liberation." This declaration was also signed by the Socialist Unity Party of the GDR.

Ion Iliescu wanted to deceive the Romanians about the fact that in the „Front of National Salvation" there were many old communist henchmen as well as some intellectuals. He felt that he was the intellectual leader he had appointed himself to be. He formed networks to consolidate his power. He called the National Salvation Party a party of incorruptibles.

An anonymous group calling itself the „Committee for National Change within the Framework of the Romanian Communist Party" issued a 44-point program in late 1989 calling for the entire Ceaușescu clan to be ousted and imprisoned.

In January 1990, numerous intellectuals had left the „Front of National Salvation" and gone into opposition to Iliescu (Doina Cornea, Mihai Caramitru and the pastor Laszlo Tökes). They felt abused by Iliescu.

Members of the National Salvation Front, Ceaușescu's closest associates, began publishing alleged plots against Ceaușescu and their part in his overthrow in May 1990. A few months earlier, they had been chanting „Ceaușescu-Ceaușescu our Titan" in the National Assembly. The Grand National Assembly had 369 members. They were composed as follows: 47% workers, 41% intellectuals and 11.5% peasants.

Cooperation between Iliescu and Prime Minister Petre Roman proved very difficult. Behind Iliescu stood the old nomenklatura, and behind Petre Roman stood younger technocrats. They had not held high office during the Ceaușescu dictatorship, but they were sons of the nomenklatura who had never suffered material hardship.

President Iliescu wanted a French-style presidential system. Prime Minister Roman, on the other hand, advocated a political system with a strong prime minister. The president should have only representative powers.

Petre Roman was free of the baggage of the communist nomenklatura. Justice Minister Victor Babiuc advocated a „trial" of communism in February 1991. Prime Minister Roman called for the top leaders of the former party and the security apparatus to be brought to trial. He did not want a sham trial, but a judicial trial. His plans were not realized.

Iliescu miners and students

Ion Iliescu was elected by the population not as a member of the former communist nomenklatura, but as a liberator from communism.

After the overthrow of the Ceaușescu regime in 1990, students protested against the seizure of power by the old communist Iliescu and his clique. Police cars and buildings burned in București. Iliescu and his clique staged this chaos to fake a coup d'état. Iliescu then mobilized miners, who bloodily crushed the protests with pickaxes on June 15, 1990.

For weeks, students had peacefully demonstrated and declared the square a „neo-communist free zone." Thousands of București residents gathered in the city center as they realized that Romania was taking a wrong turn. Many felt that the revolution had been stolen and that the old communist Ion Iliescu had usurped power. He not only rejected democratic structures, he fought them deeply.

Iliescu thanked the miners with the following words: „My dear miners, I thank you for this solidarity reaction of the working class."

16. Departure to democracy

The court case opened against Iliescu at the end of November 2019 was surprising. Previously, those formerly in charge were not to be held accountable. Iliescu was president of Romania from December 1989 to 1996 and from 2000 to 2004. He was accused of committing crimes against humanity during the Romanian Revolution in 1989.

The importance of the trial cannot be overstated. To this day, it is disputed whether the events in December 1989, when 1,100 people lost their lives, were actually a revolution or a coup d'état.

Unfortunately, Romania's civil society has not been able to hold the culprits of the Ceaușescu era accountable for what happened then.

The old cadres of the Securitate and the national-fascist cadres it trained continue to have an enormous influence on Romania to this day.

17. 1965 – 1989 Functional Elites in Romania

Gabanyi describes the following in her standard work „System Change in Romania": By 1964, due to a general amnesty, numerous scientists and artists had been released. They had been sentenced to imprisonment, labor camps and forced residence in 1947.

- In 1965, the criterion of professional competence played a greater role in the selection of new leadership elites than age or length of membership in the Communist Party.

- In the early 1980s, the use of photocopiers was made subject to state control.

- The travel of state artists and scientists to Western countries and contacts with their Western colleagues were restricted in the early 1980s.

- Over time, nationally-minded members of the army had come to realize that Ceaușescu's ruinous economic and foreign trade policies posed a threat to national security. Military merit elites were aggrieved that their prominent position had been curtailed by the Securitate.

- Dissatisfaction with Ceaușescu united bureaucrats, old enemies and old friends of the dictator. The forced industrialization, to the detriment of agriculture, led to resistance to Ceaușescu's political directionality. In politics, according to Romanian political scientist Gabriel Ivan, the nomenklatura has played no social role since the early 1980s.

- Officers sent to the reserves early or transferred to the civilian economy in 1978, 1983, and 1985 formed a protest potential that cooperated with Ceaușescu's hostile functional elites in the party and security apparatus.

- Ceaușescu's ruinous economic and foreign trade policies were also seen as a threat to national security. Gabanyi reports that in 1968 Ceaușescu appointed his brother, military historian General Ilie Ceaușescu, as chairman of the Supreme Political Council of the Army. His role in overthrowing the dictatorship is one of many mysteries that led to the 1989 revolution.

- Since 1985, a few months after Michael Gorbachev took office, Russia has been involved in several attempts to overthrow Ceaușescu, according to Gabanyi.

- In 1988, however, it was not only the meritocracy within the party that rebelled. In the 1980s, Ceaușescu also went on a collision course with the party apparatus.

- Party officials were well aware of the threat to their statute and privileges posed by Ceaușescu. As early as 1984, disguised purges took place in the party, as well as numerous reshuffles at the top of the apparatus. The pent-up resentment explains why Ceaușescu had so little support in the apparatus in December 1989.

- By rotating the party leaders, Ceaușescu wanted to prevent representatives of the nomenklatura from building their own networks and forming centers of power.

- Over the years, power was reduced to a smaller and smaller circle of officials, much to the detriment of the younger technocratic elites. The ruling elite included family members and individuals who were personally sworn to Ceaușescu. This was not the case to the same extent in the other Eastern Bloc countries.

- Ceaușescu could no longer maintain the client system, which flourished in good times, in difficult economic times. Therefore, tensions arose within the communist apparatus. The security forces could no longer suppress the uprising, which led to revolution.

- During 1989, discrepancies arose between the military and Ceaușescu . For this reason, Ceaușescu refused the customary promotion of deserving military personnel on August 23, 1989, then Romania's national holiday.
- With the fall of the Soviet Union, Ceaușescu could no longer count on the support of the other communist states in Eastern and Southeastern Europe.
- In the GDR, Hungary, Czechoslovakia and Bulgaria, there was talk of a peaceful revolution; only in Romania was it bloody.
- Communism ended in the communist Eastern Bloc countries as follows:
- GDR: The end of the GDR was already sealed when it did not even exist. At the Potsdam Conference in the summer of 1945, all Allies assumed that Germany would be unified. In this respect, its later division was a consequence of the Cold War.
- Poland: On July 4, 1989, the Polish opposition movement Solidarnosc won the election against the ruling Communists. On January 1, 1990, the renaming of the People's Republic of Poland as a socialist state was changed in favor of the designation „democratic constitutional state." Polish Prime Minister Jaruzelski had already spoken with Michael Gorbachev in 1986 about the necessary reforms in the Eastern Bloc. His analysis: Ceaușescu does not want to carry out any reform in Romania and the other Eastern Bloc leaders are old and retarded.
- Hungary: After the dissolution of the People's Republic of Hungary, Mátyás Szűrös became the first president of the Republic of Hungary on October 23, 1989.
- CSSR: In mid-November 1989, a reform program by Michael Gorbachev led to demonstrations lasting several days in Bratislava and Prague as well. As a result, the communist leadership resigned.

At the end of December 1989, the writer and civil rights activist Václav Havel was elected president.

- Bulgaria: On January 15, 1990, the Bulgarian Communist Party deleted its claim to leadership from the constitution. The end of the socialist era was ushered in by free elections to a constituent People's Assembly in 1990.
- Albania: Albania was the last state in Eastern Europe in which the Iron Curtain fell. On March 31, 1990, Albania held its first democratic elections.
- USSR: After the resignation of Michael Gorbachev on December 25, 1991, the last president of the USSR, its existence ended. The dissolution of the world's largest socialist state also marked the end of the Cold War.

17.1 Transformation – Development since 1989

As Gabanyi reports in her analysis of systemic change in Romania, „power grabs" occur after mass mobilization through a successful overthrow of ruling elites, through new elites and a change in structures.

There were 7 days between the beginning of the demonstrations in Timişoara on December 16, 1989 and his capture. His execution took place 3 days later.

On December 31, 1989, all the violent clashes were over. Romania was the only country in East-Central Europe where violence was used: 1104 people died and 3352 people were injured.

The legitimization of the new leadership was the execution of Ceauşescu's. As before, the available sources are not accessible to the public.

The Eastern European changes would not have been possible without the support of the electronic media. Gabanyi calls them radio and telerevolution. They led to the delegitimization of the leaders in their countries. The dissemination of news by Deutsche Welle, BBC, Radio

Free Europe and the Voice of America were essential. Through the tele-revolution, the communist states had lost their sovereignty over information.

A century of upheaval followed in Europe. Since 1989, the bourgeois pluralist democracy of the market economy has prevailed over the failed central political socialism of the bureaucratic party dictatorship. The restoration of communist socialism has become unlikely. Whether democracy or an authoritarian system will be established in Romania in the long term is uncertain. We see that 25 % of the Romanian population mourns Ceaușescu.

17.2 Post-Communist Era 1990-1992

The legacy of 44 years of communist dictatorship could not be abruptly eliminated. Unlike Poland, Romania, the Czech Republic and Slovakia, membership in the Communist Party was usually the prerequisite for higher education, a good job and travel abroad to the communist states. The ubiquitous Securitate had undermined normal, social and political relations.

After 1989, more than 200 new political parties emerged in Romania that were more about people than programs. All of the larger parties advocated democracy and market reforms. The ruling National Salvation Front (FSN) sought to protect all former members of the government and the Securitate. It also advocated slower economic reforms.

After the fall of communism in 1989, the structures of the Securitate remained intact. The same people worked for the newly created internal service. Thus, in Romania, Iliescu and his followers were able to continue running the country. He had the ability to form networks. This is how he secured his power.

Iliescu and his followers have been doing everything since 1989 to deceive the following generations by trying to rewrite history.

Opposition parties

The National Liberal Party PNL and the Christian Democratic Peasants' Party PNȚ-CD favored rapid and radical reforms and immediate privatization of industry. They hoped to contain the influence of the Communists.

The old communist party „RKP" had dissolved, but many former party members remained active in its network.

Presidential and parliamentary elections were held on May 20, 1990. The FSN (Front of National Salvation) received 66.31 % of the votes and thus three quarters of the seats in parliament. The strongest opposition parties were the Democratic Alliance of Hungarians in Romania (UDMR) with 7.23 % and the PNL with 6.41 %.

As anti-communist workers and students faced continued political and economic influence from former leading members of the Ceaușescu era, anti-communist demonstrators met in București University Square for a standing protest.

The FSN split into two groups in March 1992, led by Ion Iliescu (FDSN) and Petre Roman (FSN). Roman's party subsequently took the name Democratic Party (PD).

17.3 Developments since 1992 to the present day

1992-1996

The local and national elections in September 1992 showed the political divide between the city and the rural population. The rural population was grateful for the return of the agricultural land. This was returned to the peasants after it had been taken away from them under Gheorghiu-Dej and Ceaușescu. Therefore, the peasants favored President Ion Iliescu's FDSN, while the urban population voted for the PNT, the PNL and some civic organizations because they advocated rapid reforms.

Iliescu was elected again in 1992, and the FDSN won a majority in both houses of parliament. The FDSN formed a government under Nicolae Văcăroiu in November 1992, with parliamentary support from the nationalist PUNR and PRM parties and the communist PSM.

In July 1993, the FDSN was dissolved and henceforth called itself the „Party of Social Democracy of Romania" (PSDR). The PSDR, which later called itself the PSD (Partidul Social Democrat), is a socialist party that has nothing to do with the social democratic parties of northern or western Europe.

1996-2000

The 1996 local elections led to a reorientation of the Romanian electorate. The opposition parties won the elections in București, in the large cities in Transylvania and in Banat.

The trend continued in the 1996 national elections, with the opposition winning in the cities and also in rural areas. The opposition had focused on the issues of fighting corruption and economic reform. This promise resonated with the electorate, and Emil Constantinescu and the parties allied with him came to power.

Emil Constantinescu of the „Democratic Convention of Romania" (CDR) won against the ruling President Iliescu by a margin of 9% and became the new President of the Republic.

In an interview (Le Monde, Feb. 22, 1997), seven years after the end of the Ceaușescu dictatorship, he declared, „It is our ambition to preserve the functionaries and the state companies of the old regime. We want to pursue an independent and anti-Western policy that prevents all changes to our system by European and non-European countries."

In 2012, Dan Voiculescu, former Securitate employee and current top Romanian politician, stated, „We old Securitate officials still don't have all the power if we don't take all the justice."

The socialist PSDR won the most seats in Parliament. The Democratic Party, the PNL, the CDR and the Democratic Union of Hungarians of Romania (UDMR) together formed a coalition government. Victor Ciorbea became prime minister and ruled until March 1998, when he was succeeded as prime minister by Radu Vasile (PNȚ-CD) and then by the head of the National Bank, Mugur Isărescu.

The influence of former communists and members of the Securitate was limited during this period of government. Furthermore, decisions were made for a functioning market economy.

The coalition government formed in December 1996 took a historic step by forming a coalition with the Hungarian UDMR party.

2000-2004

The socialist PSD (Party of Social Socialists) and Ion Iliescu won the parliamentary elections in November 2000. The liberal PNL and the Democratic Party were in opposition, while the Christian Democratic PNȚ-CD failed to clear the 5 percent electoral hurdle. Adrian Năstase became prime minister. In October 2003, several ministers had to resign due to allegations of corruption.

Iliescu and Năstase hindered the development of democratic structures. Since living conditions in Romania were precarious, they wanted to join the EU in order to improve living conditions in the country. The United States lobbied for Romania's membership in NATO for geopolitical reasons. It took place on March 29, 2004.

2004-2008

Presidential elections were held on November 28 and December 12, 2004. Prime Minister Adrian Năstase was the candidate of the Socialist PSD, and the mayor of București Traian Băsescu was the candidate of the D.A. Liberal Alliance. While Năstase focused on continuing his government, which had been rocked by corruption scandals, Băsescu promised to put an end to rampant corruption.

Traian Băsescu won the election and appointed Călin Popescu-Tăriceanu nu of the liberal D.A. Alliance as prime minister.

On November 28, 2004, the bicameral parliament was also newly elected. The largest faction was formed by the D.A. of PNL and PD, who formed a center-right government with PUR and UDMR. They promised to root out corruption and implement reforms in agriculture and industry.

On April 13, 2005, the European Parliament in Strasbourg approved the accession of Romania and Bulgaria to the European Union, although they had not met the requirements for membership. Romania and Bulgaria have been members of the EU since January 1, 2007.

In 2007, the alliance of the PNL and PD broke apart. However, Tăriceanu continued to govern with a minority government of the PNL and UDMR that was largely unable to act.

When Brussels raised the democratic deficits in Romania in 2008, Crin Antonescu declared that Romania is not a colony. Money from the EU is demanded, but no interference in Romanian affairs.

2008-2011

In 2008, Romania held parliamentary elections independently of the presidential elections. The socialist PSD and the newly formed PD-L won the elections and appointed Emil Boc as prime minister. Harsh austerity measures and reduced social benefits led to protests in Romania. The Boc II cabinet resigned as some deputies left the ruling PD-L party, especially since they were made lucrative offers by the opposition party.

President Traian Băsescu appointed Mihai Răzvan Ungureanu as prime minister in early February 2012 and entrusted him with forming a government. He failed after only a few months following a vote of no confidence by the socialist PSD and PD-L parties.

A new coalition government was formed under Prime Minister Victor Ponta to oust Romanian President Traian Băsescu. Parliament voted to suspend President Băsescu, and Senate President Crin Antonescu continued in office. Since the turnout in the election was less than 50%, the election was declared invalid.

When the EU denounced the democratic deficits in Romania, Crin Antonescu declared, „Romania is not a colony of the EU." Romania continued to expect the billions in subsidies from Brussels, but rejected any interference in Romania's internal affairs. A constant power struggle raged among political parties as officials sought to enrich themselves from EU funds.

The chief judges of the Constitutional Court of Bucureşti also reported on the enormous pressure exerted against them by the government. There was no question of an independent judiciary.

2012-2014

After less than three months in office, Ungureanu's government failed in a successful vote of no confidence in parliament brought by the socialist PSD and the PD-L. The government's success in the parliamentary elections was the result of a vote of no confidence in Ungureanu's government.

Defectors from the National Liberal Party (Romanian: Partidul Național Liberal, PNL), the Social Democratic Party (Partidul Social Democrat, socialist PSD) and the Conservative Party (Partidul Conservator, PC) joined forces to form a new governing alliance: the Social Liberal Union (Uniunea Social Liberală, USL) under Prime Minister Victor Ponta. The declared goal was to oust Romanian President Traian Băsescu of the PD-L. Impeachment proceedings against Băsescu were initiated in late June 2012. The parliamentary vote led to the president's suspension. The official duties were continued by the national-liberal Senate President Crin Antonescu. In the July 29, 2012 referendum to impeach Băsescu, many PD-L supporters responded to the call to boycott the election. Since the turnout was below the required 50 % of possible votes, it was declared invalid. Of the votes cast, around 87 % had opted for impeachment.

The USL's approach has been described by critics as a „coup d'état" and drew national and international criticism. In addition to widespread corruption in Romania, there is a power struggle between the politician cliques of the various camps.

2014-2021

Since joining the EU in 2007, Romania has been under special scrutiny by the EU Commission because it failed to meet targets for fighting corruption and organized crime and strengthening the judiciary. Romania is considered one of the most corrupt countries in Europe. The EU Commission therefore publishes annual progress reports. The Romanian governments arbitrarily changed constitutional laws, and the EU criticized serious deficits in the rule of law and democracy. Several Romanian courts asked the European Court of Justice whether the progress reports were mandatory. In response, the EU Commission informed Romania that it had undertaken to comment on these progress reports before the country's accession.

In 2014, President Klaus Johannis, the mayor of Sibiu, was elected as Băsescu's successor.

The demonstration in București led to the resignation of Ponta's government on November 4, 2015. Sorin Cîmpeanu became interim minister.

On November 4, 2015, Ponta announced his resignation. This was preceded by days of protests and demonstrations with over 20,000 participants in București against Ponta's government. The wave of protests was triggered by the devastating fire in a București nightclub on October 31, 2015, which claimed over 60 lives. The simplest safety regulations were ignored. The nightclub owner had bought his operating license through bribes. Sorin Cîmpeanu, the former education minister, was named interim head of government.

Viorica Dăncilă (Socialist PSD) held office between January 29, 2018 and November 3, 2019, and her two predecessors, Sorin Grindeanu and Mihai Tudose, were ousted by the usual internal power struggles within the Socialist PSD.

On January 4, 2017, Sorin Cîmpeanu of the socialist PSD became prime minister. He intended to stop hundreds of cases against politicians. After the publication on January 31, 2017, of an order for an amnesty, demonstrations against the government took place daily in Bucureşti and other cities. In Bucureşti alone, about 450,000 democratically-minded Romanians protested against the planned amnesty legislation on February 1 and about 500,000 on February 5. It was the largest mass protest in the history of Romania. The author of this paper participated in a demonstration of the Romanians abroad in Stuttgart. These protests received worldwide attention. On February 14, 2017, the Senate and on February 21, the Romanian Parliament spoke out against the planned decree to stop the proceedings against corrupt politicians.

According to a 2021 survey, 70-75 % of Romanians do not trust political parties, parliament or the government. They believe they have no influence on political decisions. Young people are interested in fashion, theater and video games, just not in politics. In the seminars on intercultural communication in Cluj-Napoca, students were advised just not to choose a political topic. While the older generation in Romania still votes because they still experienced the lack of freedom of the communist system, the younger generation lacks this awareness of the problem. If this remains the case, democracy in Romania is at risk, as is membership in the EU in the long term. Absentee voting does not exist in Romania. Young students can only vote at their main place of residence, usually at their parents' house. Since they would have to travel home to vote, they give up their right to vote.

17.4 Herta Müller, German-Romanian Nobel Prize winner

I would like to trace the career of Herta Müller, a Romanian patriot.

- She was born a Banater Swabian in the Banat. Her grandfather was a wealthy farmer and his property was expropriated during the Ceaușescu dictatorship. Her mother was deported to a Soviet camp in Ukraine after World War 2 for several years of forced labor because she had German ancestors.

- Between 1960 and 1968 she attended the German school in Nițchidorf. She then attended the German-language Nikolaus Lenau Lyceum in Timișoara, where she properly learned the Romanian language. After graduating from high school, she studied German and Romance languages and literature at the University of Timișoara from 1973 to 1976.

- From 1976 she worked as a translator in a machine factory. She was asked several times by the Securitate to work as an informer for the Securitate. She refused to do so because, as she said, „she does not have that character." As a result, she was accused by the director of the machine factory of working for a foreign secret service.

- In 1984, Herta Müller moved to Germany with her husband. Herta Müller received a number of teaching assignments abroad: in 1998 she became a visiting professor at the University of Kassel, in 2001 at the University of Tübingen, and in 2005 at the Free University of Berlin. In 2008 she was awarded the Nobel Prize and in 2010 the Grand Cross of Merit with Star of the Federal Republic of Germany and many other awards for her life's work.

In 2018, I attended a lecture by her in Salzburg. During the discussion, I made the suggestion to Ms. Müller to also give a lecture at a Romanian university about the crimes of the Ceaușescu dictatorship. Her reaction: „In my country of birth, Romania, I am considered a nest-dirtier."

The mindset in Germany is thankfully different: Willy Brandt fled the Nazis as a 20-year-old and fought them. He later became Chancellor of the Federal Republic of Germany, one of the great role models of this country.

This shows the difference in mindset between a misunderstood democracy in Romania and a lived democracy in Western Europe.

As long as Romania does not accept the German-Romanian winner of the Nobel Prize for Literature, Herta Müller, as an icon of freedom, Romania will have no future.

17.5 Laura Codruța Kövesi, Prosecutor General in Romania

Kövesi, Laura Codruța, born May 15, 1973 in Sfântu Gheorghe, is a Romanian lawyer who headed Romania's Supreme Corruption Authority between 2013 and 2018.

Her dissertation was on the fight against organized crime. Laura Kövesi had studied law at Babeș-Bolyai University in Cluj, Lucian Blaga University in Sibiu and West University in Timișoara. After graduating from law school, she became a prosecutor in Sibiu and in 2013 took over as head of Romania's anti-corruption agency. Because Kövesi was very successful in investigating corruption, she was a thorn in the side of many corrupt politicians. On July 9, 2018, she was dismissed from this position by order of Justice Minister Tudorel Toader, despite initial opposition from President Klaus Johannis.

Communist MP Sebastian Ghiță leveled baseless corruption charges against her, which were thrown out by the country's Supreme Court. Nevertheless, Kövesi was indicted on March 28, 2019, and banned from leaving Romania. The proceedings were seen as politically motivated to prevent Kövesi's appointment as an EU general attorney. The travel and freedom restrictions were lifted by the Supreme Court on Apr. 3, 2019.

On Sept. 19, 2019, Kövesi was elected by the majority of EU states to head the EU Anti-Corruption Agency in Luxembourg and has headed the agency since June 1, 2021. The Romanian government wanted to stop the appointment, which it failed to do.

Kövesi is now considered one of the most influential personalities in Europe, according to Politico ranking: Olaf Scholz, Emmanuel Macron, Christine Lagarde, Frans Timmermans (EU Vice-President), Rishi Sunak (UK Finance Minister), Laura Codruța Kövesi (Head of the Romanian Anti-Corruption Agency between 2013-2018 and since the beginning of June 2021 the Prosecutor General of the newly launched EU Prosecutor's Office).

Kövesi declined to run for president of Romania in June 2022.

17.6 Elena Udrea, former minister

How the judiciary in Romania is obstructed by politics can be seen in the example of former minister Elena Udrea. In an article published by the online newspaper Romania Insider on April 8, 2022, the following statements are made:

On April 7, 2022, Romania's Supreme Court rejected former Development Minister (PDL/PMP) Elena Udrea's appeal against her conviction for bribery and abuse of office, upholding the earlier final judgment.

The convicted fled in her car to Bulgaria, where she was arrested on an international arrest warrant.

In 2018, Elena Udrea had absconded in the same way: then to Costa Rica, where she described herself as a „political refugee." In July 2018, the Constitutional Court's ruling against her and other former politicians was overturned after a change of government. Reason: the Constitutional Court „had been illegally formed." Udrea then returned to Romania. Since there was another change of government and another change of judges at the highest court, Udrea must now serve a six-year prison sentence and pay three million euros in reparations for the „damages."

The former mayor of Bucureşti, Sorin Oprescu, was sentenced to 10 years and 8 months in prison for corruption.
Other convictions:
- Bogdan Popa at 11 years, 6 months
- Cristian Stanca at 7 years, 2 months
- Mircea Octavian Constantinescu, 6 years, 10 months

Traian Băsescu was president of Romania between 2004 and 2014. The Securitate Archives Research Authority (CNSAS) found that he worked for the Securitate during his student days and later as a ship captain. He is to be stripped of his privileges as former president.

17.7 Gabriela Adameşteanu: The Provisional Love – Novel

In Gabriela Adameşteanu's novel, „The Provisional Love", a secret affair is described in which the Romanian secret service knows more about you than you do.

Gabriela Adameşteanu, born in 1942, is one of the intellectuals who refused to cooperate with the Securitate in Romania during the Ceauşescu period.

The novel is set in the early Ceauşescu era, in the 1960s and 1970s. It writes about World War 2, August 23, 1944, when King Mihai I. Ion Antonescu's military dictatorship overthrew and sided with the Allies against Hitler's Germany. This day decided the fate of several generations. It paved the way for communism. It was a seamless transition from military dictatorship to the communist system: people were liberated or prevented, made blackmailable. Anyone familiar with the images of Herta Müller, who describes the 1970s, knows that this state of affairs continued after 1989.

17.8 Lavinia Braniște: Sonja reports – novel

In the book „Sonja meldet sich" by Lavinia Braniște, the repression of the Ceaușescu period is addressed.
Lavinia Braniște, who was born in the late 1980s, talks about the time before her birth. Many like-minded people feel the same way.
Today there are fast food chains and galleries next to former prison cells. In these, innocent people had to suffer because they were against the Ceaușescu system. People don't want to know anything about that time. Older people I asked can't or don't want to remember. Should we condemn our parents because they did nothing? This is the central question of guilt. What did you do in the dictatorship or against it? Peers know the TV pictures of the conviction and execution of Ceaușescu and his wife. After Ceaușescu's death, life went on freely without atonement. The politicians and Securitate informers continued. Often in the same positions they held before 1989.

17.9 The silence of a generation

Louisa von Essen reports on the young people at Babeș-Bolyai University who voted in December 2020 in an article on „The silence of a generation" in Country Focus, Jan. 21, 2021.
In German political science lectures, the election results would have been a topic of conversation among the students. In Romania, young people want nothing to do with politics and do not discuss it with family and friends.
In Romania, the USR „Save Romanian Union" party was founded by people who had never been politically active before. They claim to stand for a strong judicial system, the rule of law, the fight against corruption, transparency and for fundamental European values. This population group is dissatisfied with the democratic stagnation in the country. But it is also an expression of a divided society. On the one hand, there are EU-oriented, well-educated citizens from București, Cluj-Napoca, Brașov or Iași. On the other hand, there is a conservative

rural population, especially in the south. The fact that voter turnout is so low in Romania is by no means due to the fact that the majority is satisfied with the government's measures. On the contrary, there have been remarkable anti-corruption processes, especially in the last 5 years. There have been large-scale demonstrations in many Romanian cities against the socialist PSD, which wanted to relax the criminal prosecution of corruption.

17.10 Civil society in Romania

Since 2007, Dr. Roxana Stoenescu has been a lecturer at the Department of International Relations and German Studies at Babeș-Bolyai University in Cluj-Napoca.

In an interview with Michael Mund, of the German General Newspaper in Romania (ADZ) on May 9, 2018, Dr. Roxana Stoenescu described the development of Romanian civil society as follows:

Romanian civil society is only at the beginning of its development. Until now, civil society has always been associated with the labor movement, such as the Mineriads. Mineriads are the name given to several violent protest actions that were carried out in Romania, mainly by miners from the Jiu valley. Romania was the only country in Eastern Europe to experience a bloody revolution. Civil society in Romania has always been associated with violence and repression.

In the beginning, there is the civil society that Jürgen Habermas used to talk about. It developed in the 19th century in Western countries with the rise of the bourgeoisie. Civil society was a movement of the middle class, not of the workers. It developed in Western Europe at the beginning of the 20th century. It was the time of industrialization, liberalism and socialism and communism in the Marxist sense. All this did not take place in Romania as it did in Poland, Czechoslovakia and Hungary. In these countries, there was already partial liberalization before 1989.

This was not possible in Romania. Here, national communism or socialism existed, as demonstrated by Ceaușescu's austerity policies. Romania went its own political way and was one of the few Eastern Bloc countries against which the Soviet Union did not take military action. It was not a country occupied by the Soviet Union, as had happened in the case of the other satellite states. There was no „foreign" power to oppose, but the „own repressive power" and the „own national communist party", and not that of the Soviet Union. Therefore, resistance and opposition were not as strong as in other Eastern Bloc countries. Communism in Romania was also the heyday of Romanian nationalism. People could identify with it and therefore tolerated it. Romanian communism used political myths, such as those of the Daco-Romanian continuity theory, to emphasize Romanians as a nation. They considered themselves Christians of Europe who had already fought „eternally at the gates of Europe against the barbarians of the Orient." For the first time, a national pride could develop in Romania.

Quite deliberately, the structures of the minorities were broken up. After schooling or vocational training, people were sent to work in other cities. Moldovans came to Brașov, and Romanians of Hungarian origin from Szeklerland had to go to Moldova or to the south of the country. This was to prevent or disintegrate communal groupings such as existed among minorities. Thus, no real sense of community could develop among the Romanians either.

Among the Romanians, a national feeling developed, but not a sense of community. They wanted/needed to see themselves as an old nation. However, the communist party and the Securitate only sowed mistrust and hostility among the population in order to prevent oppositional unions.

The student revolts showed that there was no democracy under Ion Iliescu either. Civil society developed only to a very limited extent until Romania joined NATO in 2004 and the EU in 2007. The European Court of Human Rights has therefore repeatedly criticized Romania for massively restricting freedom of expression. Journalists who publicly voiced criticism were threatened with prison sentences, which greatly intimidated the population. Moreover, the Securitate has been almost completely taken over by the „Serviciul român de informații" (SRI), the Romanian secret service. There was no new beginning, no changes: The same people were still active in the secret service, in political parties, in business and in the media.

The massive unemployment after the collapse in 1989 made the Ceaușescu dictatorship appear in a better light in people's memories. People experienced renewed poverty, did not feel liberated and could do nothing with democracy.

Therefore, the next generation could not even deal with the parent generation. In the families, little is said about the communist period. Hannah Arendt said that trauma from total domination and dictatorships cannot be seen. People are not aware of the communication blockages caused by psychological suffering. Only now young students are showing interest in communism, although communism is hardly covered in school lessons.

It takes six years to convert the economy from a planned economy to a market economy.
But it takes 60 years to bring about a change in people's mentality. This means that the change in the Romanians' mentality began with their accession to the EU in 2007 and should be completed by 2067, i.e. in 45 years.

The first major protest movement took place in 2002 against the gold mining project in Roșia Montană. Now Romanians found that they can express their opinion through a peaceful protest. Roșia Montană was a turning point in the Romanians' way of thinking.
For the first time, Romanians abroad had been involved in the election of Johannis. The fire in the club „Colectiv" was also a political and administrative disaster. The Orthodox Church's explanation: people

should have gone to church instead of to a rock concert. This divided and angered people. Today, the media report peaceful demonstrations. Unfortunately, democratic structures are still weak and people are easily influenced by populists.

The communist populists promise the people everything before the elections: higher wages, higher pensions, lower taxes. The financing of these promises does not interest the population. There are only the following financing options to keep the promises: higher taxes, borrowing by the state or higher payments from the EU.

Many Romanians are still looking for a leader figure. They do not understand that President Johannis performs only a representative function. Therefore, many Romanians are politically disoriented.

During the Ceaușescu dictatorship, the state decided everything for the people. Now they are supposed to take the initiative and take their lives into their own hands. This is very difficult, especially for the older generation.

Since 2007, civil society in Romania has developed very slowly, although urban youth have become more cosmopolitan. According to research, Romanians need a „leader" to follow. After 1989, the older generation found it very difficult to take care of their own issues. Before, everything was controlled and regulated by the state.

In the Romanian Parliament, deputies change parties as soon as they are offered a ministerial post. They think of their own careers and are not interested in the structures of a democracy.

Only 25% of young Romanians declare themselves willing to participate in demonstrations, petitions, party work or voluntary service (fire department, technical relief organization, Caritas, etc...). Communism has blocked and destroyed people's initiative. According to sociologists, it will take several generations before the majority of Romanians prefer democratic structures to a totalitarian system. In the last elections in Romania, the Communist Party obtained over 30% of the vote, more than in other European countries, with the exception of Bulgaria. The Greater Romania Party scored 19.5 % of the vote in the last election. Romania should shape its own future.

The emergence of democracy after the fall of communism in 1989-1990 took place in Romania with delays and many shortcomings. The communist successor party, the socialist PSD, „came to terms with the new political system. It is Romania's strongest party. The socialist PSD's power base is a network of „red barons" with close ties to the local economy. The bourgeois center-right is composed of the National Liberal Party (PNL). The „self-cleaning mentality" and corruption are the biggest problems on the road to a democratic polity based on the rule of law.

In the summer of 2018, thousands took to the streets in Bucureşti to protest the erosion of Romania's legal system. The ruling Socialist PSD had introduced reforms designed to weaken the judiciary and make it harder to prosecute corruption. Liviu Dragnea (Socialist PSD) was president of Romania's Chamber of Deputies from the 2016 parliamentary election until his arrest in May 2019. In 2017, he was charged by prosecutors with creating a criminal group that falsified documents to illegally obtain EU funds. Because of his criminal record, he was unable to become prime minister, but – according to observers – exercised power in Romania. In particular, he wanted to relax criminal penalties for corruption and stop court cases against corrupt politicians. He was sentenced to 3 ½ years in prison. In May 2019, the Supreme Court confirmed the prison sentence.

On January 17, 2022, Deutsche Welle reported on right-wing extremist riots against the German mayor in Timişoara. Supporters of the nationalist right-wing extremist party „Alliance for the Unification of Romanians (AUR)" gathered in the city center of Timişoara on Jan. 14, 2022, to riot against the German-born mayor Dominic Fritz.

George Simion is a Romanian nationalist who founded the AUR (Great Romanian Party). The party does not conform to European values, as it opposes minorities, same-sex marriage, masks, and vaccines.

The AUR chairman incites against the German-born mayor, who in September 2020, became the first local politician with foreign citizenship to be elected mayor of a Romanian city. Romanian journalist Christian Tudor Popescu compared the demonstration to SA marches in Germany in the 1920s and 1930s.

The mayors of 23 Romanian cities signed a declaration of solidarity for their colleague Dominic Fritz and demanded that the state take tougher action against the rioters. The leader of the liberal-green anti-corruption party Union Save Romania (USR Plus), Dacian Cioloș, wrote on Facebook: The AUR actions took place with the permission and support of Romanian state authorities.

At this point it should be noted that Octavian Ursu, who was born in 1967 in București and has lived in Germany since 1990, has been Lord Mayor of Görlitz since 2019.

Ramona Pop was born in Timișoara in 1977 and came to Germany with her parents when she was ten years old. On her mother's side, her family belonged to the Banat Swabians. Between 2016 and 2021, she was Deputy mayor of Berlin and Senator for Economic Affairs, Energy and Labor.

The AUR wants to stop the history of the European Holocaust and the murder of 250,000 Romanian Jews as well as 25,000 Roma from being taught in schools.

- ➢ It represents „pro Putin" anti-Western, anti-Semitic and anti-minority positions.
- ➢ Its chauvinist positions are directed against the Hungarian minority in Transylvania with its 1.2 million members.

In April 2022, 49.4% consider their financial situation worse than in the previous year. 43% believe that the disadvantages will increase. 24.7% worry about higher energy prices, 19.8% about the conflict with Ukraine, and 16.3% worry about the COVID epidemic.

An insightful article appeared in the Neue Züricher Zeitung on October 26, 2021, about Romania's Western ties, which are deeply opposed by the Church and academia.

Russia is increasingly forcing national and religious ties with Romania. In Bukovina lies Putna, a national monastery. Ștefan the Great, prince of Moldavia, venerated as a saint since 1992, is buried there. Also in 2021, Daniel, patriarch of the Romanian Orthodox Church, and Aurel Pop, president of the Romanian Academy, met here at a memorial service. They applauded student leader Silvian Emanuel Man, who proclaimed the following in pathetic terms: „Romania no longer belongs to Romanians, we must take it back."

In Romania, the Church and science are held in high esteem. A look at the history of the Romanian Legionary Movement shows the following:

- ➢ The Legionary Movement was a fascist-nationalist-orthodox mass organization that fascinated intellectuals, clerics, peasants and workers.
- ➢ Nicolae Ceaușescu adopted many theses of this movement:
  - Glorification of the Romanian past
  - Xenophobia and hostility towards minorities
  - Rejection of the West
  - Economic independence

In the December 2020 elections, the ultranationalist AUR party came to the fore. With Russian support, it challenges Romania's Western ties, which were completed after the country joined NATO in 2004 and the EU in 2007.

Since the fall of Ceaușescu, the representatives of the post-communist camp have carried on the national, anti-Western ideology. Now the

AUR is back in parliament, spreading the theses of Vadim Tudor (1949-2015).

Since the 19th century, Romania has struggled to position itself between the East and the West.

The Orthodox Church has three streams:

➢ The western connection is critically accepted
➢ An orthodox state religion is advocated, which is particularly directed against minorities
➢ An open Russia friendly group

According to the NZZ article of October 26, 2021, the Patriarch Daniel and the current Academy President Ioan-Aurel Pop maintained close relations with the Securitate during the Ceaușescu dictatorship. They represent the same theses and form a network.

As V. Pabst analyzes in the NZZ of December 11, 2021, Romania has been demanding for years that more attention be paid to the alliance of the Black Sea region.

The Romanian government hopes for a stronger U.S. military presence. President Johannis has also asked allies to send a stronger troop presence to the Carpathian state. The annexation of Crimea has moved Russia's border a good deal closer to Romania. The westernmost tip is only 230 km from the mouth of the Danube River in Romania. It is 400 km from the Russian naval base of Sevastopol to the largest Romanian port of Constanța. A few years ago, Putin declared, „Our Russian armored units are capable of reaching București within 24 hours."

Since the Russian-Georgian war of 2008, București has been closely monitoring the balance of power in the Black Sea region. Iulian Fota, the security expert of the Romanian Diplomatic Institute, explained: „When Russia wants to demonstrate power, it does so in the Black Sea region, which is also a bridge to the Balkans and Syria".

At the Warsaw Summit in 2016, it was decided to deploy four multinational combat units to Poland and the Baltic states. A multinational brigade was created for the Black Sea region at Romania's insistence.

In Romania, the military enjoys an excellent reputation in contrast to the corruption-prone authorities with their notorious administrative weaknesses. That is why Afghanistan veteran and former general Nicolae Ciuca was appointed head of government on November 25, 2021.

President Johannis' PNL has reached an agreement with the Hungarian Party to form a coalition with the socialist PSD. In other words, cooperation between the liberals and the socialists, who are fighting the rule of law with all means at their disposal.

18. Review and a possible future development

After the fall of communism in 1989, the structures of the Securitate remained intact. The same people worked for the newly created domestic service. The Serviciul român de informații (SRI, Romanian Intelligence Service) is Romania's domestic intelligence service and the successor organization to the former Securitate. Thus, in Romania, Iliescu and his followers were able to continue running the country. He had the ability to form networks and thus secured his power. As reported by Romanian Insider on Aug. 3, 2022, and Deutsche Welle on Aug. 5, 2022, the military prosecutor's office has filed charges against former President Ion Iliescu, former Deputy Prime Minister Gelu Voican Voiculescu and General Ion Rus, the former head of the Romanian Air Force. The investigation is to shed light on the sequence of actions between Dec. 22 and Dec. 30, 1989.

Antonia Popescu, who as a lawyer fights for the clarification of the circumstances of that time, wants to show the young generation that Iliescu and the FSN in December 1989 were not heroes, but rather criminals.

Iliescu is accused of deceiving and deliberately misleading Romanians as head of state and government and as „head of the Council of National Salvation." Iliescu and his comrades have claimed that foreign terrorists wanted to take over violence in Romania. Investigations against Iliescu and co. have been thwarted for decades by the influence of the old Securitate clan and the Socialist Party (PSD). The European Court of Human Rights (ECHR) and the European Parliament repeatedly called on Romania to finally clarify the crimes committed by the communists against its own people.

Romania was the last communist country in Central and Eastern Europe to be swept up in the wave of political change in 1989. The reason for this was the non-existence of civil society. By that time, the other Eastern European satellite states had already made multiparty systems possible.

The conduct of these criminal proceedings against Iliescu and Co. is important for Romanian democracy. To this day, Iliescu is the honorary chairman of Romania's Socialist Party (PSD), the country's largest.

We are living today in a new turn of time. The world is being redistributed according to spheres of interest, as has always been the case in human history. Economically weak nations, like the countries of the Balkans, are financial recipient countries with a correspondingly poor ranking.

The EU has supported Romania financially since 1990, although it did not become a member until 2007. Iliescu and Co. sought to join Western Europe and the USA because economic conditions were very precarious. Although Romania did not meet the requirements for EU membership, it was admitted in 2007 at the request of the USA. Because of its long Black Sea coast, Romania became a member of NATO as early as 2004 for geopolitical reasons.
In the „Schengen State Report 2022" (May 24, 2022), the EU Commission again proposes Romania's membership in the Schengen area.

Numerous countries, as well as the USA, the EU, Switzerland, Japan, Korea, etc. have been supporting Romania financially since 1990. Thus, all schools, universities and administrative centers in Romania were built with EU funds. The same applies to the infrastructure (roads, railroad network, airports and pipelines).
Since 1990, Romania has received around 128 billion euros from the EU. In the medium term, the EU has promised Romania another 60 billion euros. EU financial support will flow to other countries (Serbia, Montenegro, Macedonia, Kosovo, Albania) in a few years to improve living conditions there.

For 32 years now, Romania has received major financial support from the EU. Romania should soon change from a net recipient to a net payer. Romania's rating would then rise sharply when Romania is no longer dependent on financial payments from EU states.

Romania has been receiving the third highest euro payments of the EU donor countries for years, after Poland and Greece. The donor countries are Germany, France, Italy, the Netherlands, Sweden, Austria, Denmark, Finland and Ireland. Therefore, the rating of the donor countries is higher than that of the recipient countries.

Some of the billions of euros made available to Romania for infrastructure were misappropriated. In part, they seeped into the pockets of Romanian „businessmen" who, together with politicians from various parties, embezzled the funds.

As reported by the „Romanian Insider" on June 3, 2022, each government promises to build new hospitals. Now two hospitals in Iași and Cluj-Napoca are in the „planning phase".

Only help through self-help leads a country further. In other words, buy a fisherman nets and do not provide him with fish cans, otherwise he will get used to the handouts for generations. If a country is dependent on financial aid from abroad, their ability to make decisions is also enormously limited. Romanians are not told this by politicians and many Romanians are not aware of it.

Economic relations: Romania is one of the fastest-growing economies in Eastern Europe. Germany is the largest foreign trading partner and investor in Romania. This is represented by big names such as Lidl, Kaufland, Daimler, Schaeffler, Continental, Miele, etc.. Since 2006, Germany has been Romania's most important trading partner. German companies generated around 27 billion euros in 2020, i.e. 13% of Romania's domestic product.

In 2020, German companies invested 13.8 billion in Romania. According to the Romanian Central Bank, most of the money went into the construction of new and modern production facilities and into companies or mergers.

Romania's accession in 2007 has proved economically beneficial. Companies from Romania conduct around three-quarters of their foreign trade with partners from EU member states. As a result of EU support programs since 1990, the state has invested in the expansion of transport routes (roads, highways, rail network, airports), power lines and broadband networks.

In recent years, Romania has developed from an „extended workbench" into an investment location for the German economy. Around 75 % of

Romania's industrial production is exported: 23 % to Germany, 10.8 % to Italy, 6.7 % to France.

List of countries by exports of goods and services worldwide:

No. 1: People's Republic of China No. 5: France
No. 2: USA No. 6: Great Britain
No. 3: Germany No. 7: Netherlands
No. 4: Japan
Luxembourg ranks 37th, even though the country has only 630,000 inhabitants.
Romania is in 42nd place.

In 2020, 21.9 of Germany's total population of 81.9 million had a migration background. This corresponds to a share of 26.7 % of the total population.
Since 1955, millions of foreigners have emigrated to Germany, changing the country. There are not too many things that have changed Germany more than the influx of foreigners. Germany's high standard of living is also due to the millions of foreign immigrants, something that is unfortunately often forgotten.
The proportion of foreigners in Romania is only 0.5 %. This is the lowest percentage of foreigners in the EU. The nationalist Simion from the AUR does not seem to understand anything about a globalized world, as he wants to reduce the proportion of foreigners in Romania even further.

According to surveys, 70% of Romanians believe that they are protected by NATO. The statement of the Socialist Defense Minister Vasile Dîncu in December 2021 was surprising: „Romania should work out its security strategy with Russia and not against Russia.

Even with the **Erasmus program,** the mindset in Romania seems to be different than in Germany.
The Erasmus program results in foreign students who study in Germany either staying in Germany or returning to their home country. As studies show, they then have strong ties in their home countries to

Germany, where they studied. This is then also reflected in political and economic relations.

The percentage of foreigners at Romanian universities is the lowest in the EU.

During a meeting in May 2020 between the EU Commissioner and the Romanian Minister of Labor Budai, the latter stated that between 4 and 5 million citizens have been educated in Romania and today contribute to the economic performance of other European countries. On the other hand, many Romanians also receive social benefits in the EU without ever having worked in the EU.

Germany also loses about 250,000 well-educated young workers per year, who seek a new future in the USA, Canada, Australia, etc.. These countries only accept educated immigrants. Bulgaria and Albania are also „bleeding out", according to UN reports. The demographic change has existed since the migration of peoples.

The statements of the Romanian socialist PSD are misleading. The question arises as to why so many Romanians vote for them.

The reason seems to be that everything is promised: higher wages, of course, an increase in child benefits and another extensive social program. What does the counter-financing look like?

Who is to generate these financial resources? There are the following possibilities: higher taxes on employees, foreign debt or a higher inflow of EU funds.

The socialist PSD wants to tax the investments of foreign investors in Romania. Then the foreign investors will not invest in Romania, but in other countries.

Freedom of the press: In 2017, around 500,000 committed Romanians protested against the corruption and abuse of power by the left-wing Ponta government. Romania is ranked 44th in press freedom, behind Burkina-Faso, Taiwan and South Korea. Yet freedom of the press, along with the independence of the judiciary, is one of the foundations of a parliamentary democracy.

Most Romanian newspapers are funded by the various political parties. The Council of Europe (CoE) has raised concerns: Romania's political parties support the media (newspapers and TV stations), by which they are supposed to be well rated.

Meanwhile, the media have become the „mouthpieces" of the political parties on which they are financially dependent.
Therefore, the Council of Europe demands disclosure of the financial agreement between political parties and the media.
The independent Romanian Internet newspaper „Romanian Insider" has existed for 12 years and reports independently. It is not financed by any political party.

Euro introduction: Romania has been preparing for euro introduction since EU membership in 2007. The various governments promised introduction in 2012, 2015, 2017 and 2019, but because the budget deficit and inflation rate are too high, introduction of the euro is completely illusory.
Before Romania adopts the euro, it must first officially join the ERM-II exchange rate mechanism and meet the Maastricht criteria.
In late summer 2017, Romania's Foreign Minister Teodor Meleşcanu announced that Romania would adopt the euro in 2022. Now, entry into the euro is planned for 2028.

Some countries in the EU are not interested in basic democratic values, but only in the financial contributions of the donor countries.
According to surveys, there are still about 25-30 % supporters of the Ceauşescu system in Romania, as well as 25 % supporters of the Greater Romania Party (nationalists). They form networks and are represented in all the country's institutions, including state agencies and universities. In 2017, about 500,000 Romanians protested in Bucureşti against corruption and for the rule of law. They were able to achieve little because they are in the minority and the old clans still make the decisions with politicians from some parties.

Only 25 % of young Romanians declare themselves willing to participate in demonstrations, petitions, party work or volunteer service (fire department, technical relief organization, Caritas). Communism has blocked and destroyed people's initiative. According to sociologists, it will take several generations before the majority of Romanians prefer democratic structures to a totalitarian system. In the last elections in Romania, the socialist PSD won over 30% of the vote, more than in any other state in Europe, with the exception of Bulgaria. The Greater Romania Party scored 19.5 % of the vote in the last election. Romania should shape its own future. Since 1989, Romania has received 128 billion euros in financial aid from the EU. Starting in 2026, funding from the EU is expected to be severely cut. Romania should then be able to fend for itself after 32 years of financial support from the EU. Germany received DM 3 billion in Marshall Plan aid from the USA in 1948.

Romania's foreign debt currently amounts to 150 billion euros. According to President Johannis, Romania feels that it is a second-class NATO state because it is allegedly not sufficiently supported by NATO. Now NATO also sent Portuguese and Belgian soldiers to Romania to support the Romanian army in case of a warlike threat.

In the 1990s, it was believed that democracy and also capitalism would spread throughout the world. During the current war between Russia and Ukraine, we realize that the conflicts of the 20th century have been taken into the 21st century. The conflicts of the 20th century, the struggle for dictatorship or democracy, continue to accompany us, especially in Romania.

Europe would be helplessly at the Russians' mercy if the U.S. military left Europe. Nuclear powers of Europe: Great Britain and France.
American nuclear bombs are stored in Germany and can theoretically be used by Bundeswehr aircraft. They are used only when Germany is threatened. President Trump declared NATO dead because European NATO partners are not providing the necessary financial contributions as the Americans are. That is why he also describes some European nations as free riders unwilling to spend two percent of their GDP on the military. If President Trump or another Republican wins the U.S.

election in November 2024, there will be a reorientation of EU and NATO policy.

Four crises have completely changed the EU: The Greek financial debacle in 2010, mass immigration in 2015, the pandemic in 2020, and the Ukraine war in 2022. Financial markets, a virus, and geopolitics have emerged as the rulers.

The Germans see themselves as the losers of the development. They feel overreached, as victims and paymasters for many states in southern and southeastern Europe.

In the 2015 migration crisis, immigrants were to be distributed according to a quota. Eastern and Southeastern Europe refused to accept immigrants.

As the European Central Bank has been turning the eurozone into a debt and liability union for years, the German Federal Constitutional Court is looking into the implications. It remains to be clarified whether a debt and liability union is compatible with the German constitution.

Europe is far from being the anchor of stability it long thought it was. The EU wanted to become a role model for the world. Now everyone can see that Europe is militarily dependent on the USA.

If the European economy loses competitiveness, this strengthens the competition in Asia. The current „lurching course" in the EU is breathtaking.

We are living in a turning point. Within a few months, the old regional conflicts in the former Soviet republics flared up again: Armenia – Azerbaijan, Kyrgyzstan – Tajikistan, Moldova – Transnistria and Gaugasia, Georgia and Kazakhstan.

According to President Putin, Russia never got over the disintegration of the Soviet Union and the independence of the satellite states (GDR, Poland, CSSR, Hungary, Romania, Bulgaria, Albania).

In Romania, too, some political parties are questioning membership in the EU and NATO. This is very worrying, as Romania could then fall into the sphere of interest of Russia, China and Turkey.

31 PERSONAL REPORTS OF SOME FORMER STUDENTS OF BBU IN CLUJ-NAPOCA

31 personal accounts of some former students of BBU in Cluj-Napoca about their grandparents' and parents' experiences during the Ceaușescu period. They also describe whether the Ceaușescu dictatorship was covered in high school and university history or political science classes. I am very grateful to the former students for supporting me in the project. As the former students told me, it is a „journey into their own past" for them to record the history of their grandparents and parents.

Finally, the students report how they and their friends assess the current political situation in Romania.

In Romania, 17 former students stayed, 14 moved abroad. This is evident from the authentic reports.

No. 1: Name: Anda F.
Place of birth: Cluj-Napoca   Place of residence: Cluj-Napoca

1. How did your grandparents (grandma and grandpa) and your parents feel about the years under the Ceaușescu dictatorship?

Our family suffered front and back. Three quarters of the family had already emigrated to Germany during the war and it was very inconvenient to keep in touch, to visit each other, to telephone undisturbed or to correspond via mail. It was beneath all dignity.

Some details:

- My grandpa was in line at 4 a.m. as soon as word got out that there was „something" the next morning. Sometimes people stood outside in the freezing cold at minus 15°C. What and how much the little truck unpacked when it finally got there and you could buy something was always a surprise and usually not a positive one. Often one has queued for hours in the long line for nothing.

- It was not easy to apply for a visit visa for Germany at the German consulate in Sibiu. One had to wait for hours and hope that everything would go well.

- Cars were allowed to drive on the roads on Sundays depending on the license plate (even/odd numbers). At the same time, there was almost no gasoline.

- There was fuel on ration, bread with food stamps, the same was true for milk.
- The state gave you a job in a village or, with vitamin B and a lot of luck, a job in the city. The early years were never master years. Even if you had studied for the teaching profession and you were good, it could happen that you ended up in a village. That is, in village A of the world, where the outhouse was in the backyard of the schoolyard. Most places

in Romania did not have a sewer system until the late 1990s, i.e., after the Ceaușescu dictatorship.

- In the summer I went to the market with grandma to sell summer apples. There was no money. Heating was partly with wood. Gas from Russia could not be relied upon, or the gas pressure was often too low.

- Living in the village was usually better. You could grow vegetables and had 1 or 2 pigs and chickens on the farm. In winter, they slaughtered to have something on the „Christmas table". One shared sometimes a pig with relatives and friends. In autumn, tomatoes, cucumbers and white cabbage were brought in. One had then a „sour" side dish for cold winter days, which is still common today.

- When my grandmother's friend sent women's magazines (Frau aktuell) from Germany every few months, there was always a copy missing. The postal workers thought of themselves, too. The same was the case with packages of groceries. Two packages for you, one for me. This was in principle so.

- Oranges and bananas were only available 1x in winter.

- Homework was often written by candlelight. When the electricity was gone for a few hours, the following joke was heard: The electricity is needed for the construction of the parliament building in București – Casa Poporului.

- Our neighbors always listened at the fence as soon as visitors from abroad arrived.

- Baptisms and religious events were rarely, if ever, allowed: then only in the Orthodox Church.

- The worst thing was: one had NO FREEDOM, and was continuously persecuted in all situations of life.

- I often think about the fact that my grandmother and her sister (of Hungarian/Saxon German origin) had to hide in a barn in the basement for a year. They were afraid of being deported to Russia. It is often said

that it was not as bad in the 70s as it was in the 40s. But I say: it was different bad!
We were lucky enough to live in a small town where there was a mix of different ethnic minorities and where great value was placed on traditions. People cultivated social contacts so that they could also enjoy life a little. In the summer, people went fishing, barbecuing or dancing. If you were lucky, you could go to the Black Sea in summer. Winters, on the other hand, were cold, long and hard.
How were the years felt: Suffering, hardship, despair and sadness.

2. Was the Ceaușescu dictatorship discussed in elementary school, high school and university?

In Romanian schools, a picture of Ceaușescu hung above the blackboard next to the teacher's desk. At 8 o'clock in the morning, before classes began, the national anthem of the time was sung. And communist poems were recited as well. In 1990 I started school and fortunately I did not experience much in my Romanian kindergarten. But even here we did not have to wear school uniforms, which was unimaginable in Romanian schools. In the German kindergarten and the German Sunday school, we had the good fortune to grow up in different cultural circles.

3. How do you and your friends assess Romania's political situation today?

The Liberals have now formed a coalition with the Social Democrats and the Hungarian party. A year ago, all the liberals were almost swearing that such a thing would never happen under them. The political crisis played out when Romania had 15,000 new Corona cases a day. Romania has 20 million inhabitants and the hospitals were collapsing. Again and again, the president stressed that it was important to finally put an end to this political crisis in order to focus on the pandemic.
Romanian politics is still dirty. The old communist doctrines and their networks are still deeply rooted among many politicians.

No. 2: Name: Adrian L.
Place of birth: Bistrița   Place of residence: Cluj-Napoca

1. How did your grandparents (grandma and grandpa) and your parents feel about the years under the Ceaușescu dictatorship?

Narration by my mother: she told me several times that she learned a lot out of great respect for the teachers. She did not go to physics class without having learned a lot in advance.

My mom came from a large family, as was the case at that time. She had 7 siblings and lived in the small village of Maieru. It was also called „little China" at that time because of the high birth rate. My mother also grew up poorly. My father had 6 siblings and came from the same village as my mother. My grandmother's mother – that is, my great-grandmother – died young. She went to school for only four years. Then she married my grandfather at some point and they then had seven children. Her husband was a tree trimmer by profession. He fell from the tree and died. She was still young and had seven children to take care of, but she never wanted to marry again.

My mother kept telling me that as the eldest daughter, she had to help raise the younger siblings. She also had to work in the house and garden. Fruits and vegetables were grown in her own garden. The animals also had to be taken care of. The field had to be mowed to have enough hay for the animals in winter.

My maternal grandparents realized that their eldest daughter, my mother, wanted to continue her education. Therefore, the decision was made that my mother should attend 7th grade in the city. Since the family had no money, my mother lived in a children's orphanage for a year. She attended a good lyceum and was then able to study chemistry. The costs were paid by the state, which I think was very good. Those were the conditions of the time. Often 5 people slept in one room. One bathroom was shared by all 5 people in the house. Hot water was only available in the morning and evening. But that was much better compared to life in the countryside. There was no water in the house, it came from the well. There was also no toilet, but an outhouse outside the house.

My mother has very fond memories of her student days. She always marvels at how my grandmother managed to take care of all the children. When my mother came home for the vacations, her mother always cooked her favorite dishes. We didn't have to go hungry. But the food was very simple: polenta with milk or potatoes with something.

I would like to answer the question of how my parents felt about life in Ceauşescu: It was ok, but my parents were probably an exception.

They came from a simple peasant family from the village. During the Ceauşescu period, intellectuals often had problems with the dictatorship.

In the region where my mother came from, it was different. During the agrarian reform between 1945 and 1962, the property of the independent farmers were expropriated. They were forced to work in the state farms. There were periods when people died of hunger. In my mother and father's home village, there was no agricultural land because it was a mountain village. I found an article that I would like to point out:

https://adevarul.ro/locale/Bistriţa/cum-fost-lasati-pamanturi-taranii-bistriteni-comunism-lipsa-terenurilor-agricole-scapat-valea-bargaului-colectivizare-1_54630ead0d133766a8c7f7c5/index.html

In the period between 1960 and 1990, there was supposedly good economic development in my parents' home village. The village population did not have to work in agricultural state farms.

My maternal grandfather was a tree trimmer, my paternal grandfather worked in the quarry. The women worked in the house and in their gardens. In the gardens and in their fields they could grow potatoes and corn, and harvest apples and plums. They were also allowed to keep some animals. Those who could cultivate their own piece of land were doing OK.

My parents' life was not easy after the Ceaușescu dictatorship. It was difficult to get a job. During the communist dictatorship, everyone was assigned a secure job after their education or after their studies. Young families were also given an apartment. After the fall of communism in 1989, ordinary people were not doing so well, as my parents told me.

In my family we had everything we needed for daily life. My parents had saved a lot so that I could also travel abroad. Nevertheless, it was difficult for my parents to afford the cost of studies for my brother and me. Now I draw a comparison with the conditions under which my mother studied. Accommodation, 3 x daily meals in the canteen, trips home, a few visits to the cinema per year and possibly two new dresses per year.

During my bachelor's and master's studies, I was always second in class. My parents gave me 150 euros a month. With this amount, I was able to pay for my accommodation in the student dormitory and for food. In addition, I could afford something new several times a year. Whenever I visited my parents, I was given „takeaway food." As a stipend, I received 60 euros per month from the university, but not during the vacations. In December, I received 50% (30 euros) because half of the month was vacation.

Of course, there are many opportunities for us now that didn't exist before 1989. But I often have the feeling that people have forgotten that there were things that were good back then. That's why I would like to list a few things: my mother will soon retire and after 40 years of work she will get less than 500 euros per month. My father, who had also studied, will receive 250 euros pension. He also worked many years, but he fell ill a few years ago.

I know that other people did not have it so good. There was often nothing to buy in the stores before 1989. Everyone was not lucky enough to have families who lived in the countryside and could help. But under communism, before 1989, people somehow managed in an ethical or unethical way:

X worked at company Y and could give goods that were not good enough for export to a friend. The friend Z, who worked at company T, gave him gasoline in return.

2. Was the Ceaușescu dictatorship discussed in elementary school, high school and university?

Yes, but I don't know that much about it.

3. How do you and your friends assess Romania's political situation today?

The current political situation in Romania is funny. You just can't believe in what you hear from politicians anymore. Today they say one thing, tomorrow they say something else. And we are all sure that politicians are also to blame for the fact that health care and education are not improving here. In cities like Cluj you already have conditions that are ok, but in villages it is terrible.

There are the former corrupt politicians who were never held accountable for their mistakes, for example Iliescu. But today's politicians also lie.

I read an interesting article a few years ago, in which they also reported on Romania after the fall of communism. It is said that there was a kind of neo-communism with its specific characteristics in Romania some years after 1989. See on this: Theodor Tudoroiu, *The Neo-Communist Regime* of *Present-Day China,* in: Journal of Chinese Political Science/ Association of Chinese Political Studies 2011.

I have some friends and also family members who work abroad. I too sometimes think of leaving Romania and working abroad.

No. 3: Name: Nelu T.
Birthplace: Braşov   Place of residence: Braşov

1. How did your grandparents (grandma and grandpa) and your parents feel about the years under the Ceauşescu dictatorship?

Life was full of restrictions during the Ceauşescu regime. The basic foodstuffs, such as meat, eggs, dairy products, exotic fruits, bananas, oranges, were made available for sale to the people only during certain hours or days. These were sold very quickly and they were also very scarce. Not everyone could get them. To be sure of getting any of them, you had to be in line as early as 4am.

I remember receiving parcels from Germany. I received these parcels from a Transylvanian-Saxon community from Germany because I had attended a German school in Romania in my childhood. This helped me a lot.

At that time there were ration cards with which you could buy food and bread. Bread was given as follows: one loaf per adult and half a loaf per child in the family. Bread and milk were rationed.

I am one of the children who had little experience of communism, because I was only 6 years old. But I still remember that we lived in fear. The rules were very hard, even for us children. We were never allowed to express our free opinion, because you quickly went to jail or you had problems with the police and the authorities. I remember when I was 6 years old I heard that Ceauşescu was dead and that we were finally free. I couldn't believe it and I was overjoyed at my young age.

Looking back, I am not nostalgic about the communist years. But like any person, I like to think back to my childhood. The children who were born before 1989 were obliged to spend a lot of time outside. They were supposed to play together, ride bikes, and hike through the woods. I have fond memories of the time I spent together with my peers. I still have lifelong friendships with some of them today. These strong friendships allow me to forget the shortcomings of the Ceaușescu years.

In those days, we had no access to technology except for the well-known video player. This video player was very difficult to acquire and cost as much as a DACIA. Romanians were constantly asked to save electricity. Pupils and students had to study and do homework in the evening with kerosene lamps. Most people had black and white television sets and old radios in their homes. You could watch television only two hours a day. We could also watch Russian cartoons and Russian movies and listen to the Romanian news. Day after day, Ceaușescu was reported on the radio and television. On television we could only see what Ceaușescu wanted or did not want. The use of refrigerators and washing machines was also limited because electricity was scarce. In winter, food was kept cold on the balcony or in the yard. These constant restrictions took away our joy of life, watching TV or listening to the radio.

The rationing of natural gas also had to be followed. People lived indoors in winter with temperatures between 16 and 20 degrees Celsius, and the heating worked only very sporadically. There was also only limited hot water for a few hours a day.

Gasoline was also rationed. Traffic was also regulated. If you had an even license plate number, you were allowed to drive on days 2/4/6, if you had an odd number on days 1/3/5/7.

People were not allowed to own property. Everything was taken away from them in the name of the state. The motto was: all people are equal. People were supposed to live in poverty. Many houses in the cities were demolished to build apartment blocks. The expropriated people were then assigned an apartment in a new apartment block. Many died of heart attacks from grief.

Even today it is said that Ceaușescu managed to pay off all foreign debts by the beginning of 1989. However, we must not forget that between 1982 and 1989 were the years of hunger for Romanians. During this period, food was rationed. The demonstrators in some cities were beaten up or murdered by the Securitate. This is also part of the truth.

2. Was the Ceaușescu dictatorship discussed in elementary school, high school and university?

In kindergarten they wore blue aprons. The school children and students also had specific uniforms, but all in dark and muted colors (blue, white, gray and black). Children aged 4 and 7 were the „Fatherland Falcons". They had to wear a uniform: orange shirt, red tie and blue pants or skirts. As for education, there was a picture of Ceaușescu in all classrooms. All children had to memorize communist poems and songs and had to honor Ceaușescu every day.

However, there were also positive aspects. There was a focus on good education for the children. Good school performance was required. If they did not study, teachers were allowed to slap the children and beat them with sticks. The parents then had to come to school, which was a big problem.

In the communist period, there were no unemployed or welfare recipients. If you didn't have a job, you were given one by the state. If you didn't want to work or if you resisted working, you went to prison.

There were also negative aspects as far as religion was concerned. Communism did not want the Orthodox Church to gain power. There was a time when people were not allowed to go to church and celebrate Christian holidays.

3. How do you and your friends assess Romania's political situation today?

The political situation in Romania is not pleasant. Hopefully war will not threaten us. God shall protect us from it! We are not happy at all about the current president and also not about the current ruling parties.

Romania has never had a good government since the monarchy. The only time when Romania was a respected country and could talk with the great European powers was during the interwar period.

Since then, no government loved their country. After the communist period, all subsequent governments have bankrupted the industry. Because everything that this country had in terms of industry was built during the Ceaușescu regime. For the industry and the factories and the development of the country, Ceaușescu did a lot for his country. He loved his country, just not his people. Companies went bankrupt or were given to foreign investors at 0 amount. Unfortunately, these investors did not use or renew the technical plants, but closed them down altogether. They did other business, but it was not for the prosperity of the country or its people.

No. 4: Name: Cosmina G.
Birthplace: Buzău   Residence: Amsterdam

1. How did your grandparents (grandma and grandpa) and your parents feel about the years under the Ceauşescu dictatorship?

I can only tell from my parents' point of view. Both of them worked in a factory during communism. I was told the following:
- there was often no electricity
- there was only access to certain foods, which were also rationed
- the quality of many products was poor
- Watching television was only possible at certain hours. There were also only certain TV shows that you were allowed to watch
- But there were also people who, because of their relationships, had a better position and could lead a better life. They had better access to better food, clothes, items, etc.
- one did not dare to say what one thought
- many people tried to leave Romania

Very many people found life under communism very difficult and they do not romanticize the period.

2. Was the Ceauşescu dictatorship discussed in elementary school, high school and university?

In high school, our history teacher told us a lot about communism. Not only during the lessons that had to do with the subject, but also on the side. In addition, we had the opportunity to choose modules where only communism and the Holocaust were taught. I chose both modules.
In the „Communism" class, in addition to the usual lessons, we watched documentaries and movies and were recommended books to read. I read these books. In the lessons, not only the history of communism in Europe and Romania was discussed. We also talked about how people's lives changed under communism. We were told and shown how the intellectuals of Romania were imprisoned and killed. The reasons for

arrest and the methods of torture were also shown. The prisons that existed at that time were also mentioned. A good book on the subject is „Fenomenul Piteşti" by Virgil Lerunca about the prison in the city of Piteşti. Unfortunately, far too little is said about this and many people are unaware of how many died during communism. Many of them were used as labor for different construction projects (example: Danube-Black Sea Canal). We were also shown how Romania's architecture has changed.

Many have lived in fear under the Ceauşescu regime. Friends, family and neighbors watched and denounced each other. It is very important to emphasize that the mentality of people changed after 1989.

3. How do you and your friends assess Romania's political situation today?

Critical. Personally, I have lost hope that anything can still change positively in politics. In my opinion, the only hope of Romania is in the still young adults who stayed in Romania. I have already left Romania, like many of my generation!!!

No. 5: Name: Breda C.
Place of birth: Târgu Mureș   Place of residence: Sibiu

1. How did your grandparents (grandma and grandpa) and your parents feel about the years under the Ceaușescu dictatorship?

My father's grandparents were born in the early 1920s and lived through the hard times of war and then the terrible years of communism.

My paternal grandmother was born and raised in Bălți (Greater Romania), now the Republic of Moldova. In 1945 she fled with her family to Sibiu. My great-grandfather had a sausage factory in his town. They left their home and their business, believing that one day they would be able to return. Unfortunately, the piece of Romania across the Prut River was conquered by the USSR and they never returned. After the Communists came to power in Romania, my great-grandmother and her family suffered from being considered „Chiabur" (Kulak) by the Communists: She was expelled from the university and she had great problems finding a job.

Great-grandfather graduated from the officer school when Romania was ruled by King Mihai I.. He married my great-grandmother and worked as an officer in Sibiu. But after a few years he was discharged from the Romanian Army because he was married to a „Chiabur" girl and refused to join the Communist Party. It was a political decision.

My father finished his medical studies in Târgu Mureș in 1985. Since he was from Transylvania, he was transferred to the southwest of the country, to Turnu Severin. At first he was housed in a room in the city's psychiatric hospital and could eat in the hospital canteen. Usually it was soup „with nothing" or some boiled potatoes or rice. He did not see meat in those days. His memories as a doctor in his early years are of hunger, cold and fear.

My great-grandfather died in 1986 and his wife was alone and sick in Sibiu. My father had to make many requests so that she could live closer to us. Only after the 1989 revolution was this possible.

Unfortunately, there are people who still speak nostalgically of that sad time of Romania.

2. Was the Ceaușescu dictatorship discussed in elementary school, high school and university?

In my opinion, the period 1945-1989 was **unfortunately** treated in a very short chapter in the history book of Romania. I could say that I personally know the communist period more from my parents' stories and books than from school. The history of Romania is only covered in 4th, 8th and 12th grade. Unfortunately, this period was discussed only very briefly. Unfortunately, I have now heard in the political debates that history and geography will no longer be taught in schools, which I would find quite tragic.

I personally believe that a people who do not know their history have problems of identification and future. At the university there was no discussion about that time.

3. How do you and your friends assess Romania's political situation today?

The situation in Romania has changed considerably since joining the European Union. Unfortunately, the current political class is still dominated by personalities who were active during the communist period or had connections to that time.

I hope and wish that the younger generations will get more involved in politics, which should lead to a new breath and a change of perspective. In these challenging times, I believe that the entire world politics has become unstable.

No. 6: Name: Panait P.
Place of birth: Orăştie   Place of residence: Sibiu

1. **How did your grandparents (grandma and grandpa) and your parents feel about the years under the Ceauşescu dictatorship?**

In our house, very little was said about the Ceauşescu dictatorship. The grandparents were rather reluctant to answer any question on my part. Most of the time there was a phrase.
Here's what I can recall off the top of my head:
- it was told that on church holidays, meetings and meetings were organized in the company so that people could not attend services in church
- I still heard that there was no unemployment. You were probably not allowed to walk freely on the street during office hours, because you were immediately asked by the Ordnungsamt where you worked. If you didn't have a job, you would have gotten one right away.

My perception is that my grandparents were without perspective and little motivation at that time. My parents were born in 1968, so they only spent their youth in Ceauşescu. I didn't hear any stories from the parents. The subject was taboo.

2. **Was the Ceauşescu dictatorship discussed in elementary school, high school and university?**

I can hardly remember hearing anything exciting about the dictatorship or Ceauşescu during school or university. A few dates, nothing else.

I then read more about the time as a young man (25+), especially in German. Thomas Kunze has told very objectively and excitingly in his work about Nicolae Ceauşescu. I am still fascinated by Romania's role in the world order of that time: mediation between the US and the Chinese and development aid to African countries. I am equally interested in how Ceaușescu negotiated with Western countries and distanced himself from the Soviet Union.

3. How do you and your friends assess Romania's political situation today?

It will probably take another generation until there is a certain „democratic maturity". My impression is that the older Romanians like it better when they get precise instructions on what to do. Without instructions, they would not know where to go and would be helpless.

I'm part of the new generation that thinks the future needs to be built here. There is still a lot of catching up to do compared to the western states, and I think we are the right people in the right place at the right time. You can make an incredible difference in Romania.

There is a general opinion that our political leaders belong to a different time and ideology. I and the people in my social environment rarely share the values of our politicians today.

I am seriously thinking of taking a short trip to North Korea in the coming years to experience a little communism „on my own skin."

No. 7: Name: Andra Z.
Place of birth: Mediaș   Place of residence: Stockholm

1. How did your grandparents (grandma and grandpa) and your parents feel about the years under the Ceaușescu dictatorship?

My grandparents stayed completely away from politics because they were very afraid. They had a farm and the property was expropriated in 1946. After they were expropriated, all the Romanian peasants of the village had to go to București in a bus. There were about 30,000 peasants who had to pay homage to Ceaușescu for the expropriation. As my grandfather told me, many peasants cried, it was sheer mockery. Their old farmhouse was destroyed and they had to live in a gray block of houses: two rooms, but no kitchen, no toilet, no shower. There was a communal kitchen in the house, the toilet was behind the house.

My grandmother died at 64 and my grandfather at 65. My father rarely speaks about this terrible time. He only told us that my grandfather's brother was in the Securitate and we were always afraid of him. After Ceaușescu's execution at the end of 1989, we wanted nothing more to do with him. But he immediately found good work in a state enterprise, because Securitate people support each other. My father said: Blood is on his hands.

2. Was the Ceaușescu dictatorship discussed in elementary school, high school and university?

When Herta Müller received the Nobel Prize for Literature in 2009, a student asked our high school teacher what it meant for Romania. His reaction: a disgrace for Romania. She is a nest-dirtier of our country and she should be banned from entering. In Germany, there is a different way of thinking. Willy Brandt became the chancellor of Germany in 1969. He fought the Nazi regime from Norway and Sweden during World War 2. Unfortunately, there is a different mindset in Romania: The negative aspects of one's own history are not told in school. Iliescu and his party wanted history classes in Romanian schools not to teach the horrors of the Ceaușescu dictatorship, even though about 100,000 Romanians were murdered in prisons and execution sites and 90,000 died in the construction of the Danube-Black Sea Canal. He also wanted the Sighet Memorial, where Romania's elite were tortured and murdered, to be razed to the ground. Unfortunately, about 25% of the population are still supporters of the Ceaușescu dictatorship today.

3. How do you and your friends assess Romania's political situation today?

Hopeless. Tragic.

How can one live in a country where Iliescu is the honorary president of the PSD? He was responsible for the shooting order issued against free Romanians in late December 1989/January 1990 who opposed the dictatorship and wanted to live in freedom. Only in Romania was the revolution bloody.

According to the data of the Institute of the Romanian Revolution of December 1989 (Institutul Revoluției Române din Decembrie 1989, IRRD), a total of 1,165 people were killed during the Romanian Revolution, 895 of them after December 22, 1989. Thousands of people were injured.

No. 8: Name: Gabriela P.
Place of birth: Cluj-Napoca   Place of residence: Ulm

1. How did your grandparents (grandma and grandpa) and your parents feel about the years under the Ceauşescu dictatorship?

My grandparents told me a lot about World War II. They told me how bad it was, how people were killed and all their belongings were stolen. Here I have to mention that two of my grandparents died very early. At that time I was 7 years old.

For my paternal grandmother it was a bad time, because they were afraid for their family. My great-grandfather was arrested in his field without warning. He was taken to a prison and had to toil as a forced laborer for 2 years. The family searched for him because no one knew where they had taken him. Many people were tortured or killed because they were against the regime.

The land was taken away from the farmers and they had to work for the agricultural collective. After the fall of communism in 1989, my grandmother had tried to get back as much land as possible through court decisions. She was the eldest sister and felt responsible for her siblings. What she got back from the state, she divided among the siblings and grandchildren.

My mother's parents were not doing very badly under communism. My grandfather had a regular job and could provide for the family. Among other things, he was a truck driver. He had forbidden my grandmother to work. He loved the traditional family structure, where the woman had to take care of the household, garden and offspring. The man was supposed to bring home the money and take care of the family. Everything was going well until the older daughter fell in love with a German whom she met on a vacation at the Black Sea. From that moment on, the whole family, including my parents, was bugged and followed by the Securitate. They had suspected that they were being bugged and therefore had not said a word about communism and the Ceaușescu regime until the fall of communism in 1989.

Professionally, my parents were not doing badly. They both studied and had a job right after graduation without having to apply or look much. As a newly married couple with a baby, they also quickly got an apartment. They were neighbors of a Securitate employee, which they only found out after the fall of communism.

Privately, the situation was not rosy:
-Electricity and heating were available only a few hours a day.
-giant queues in front of the stores around
to get   food, since everything was rationed.
- People had   money, but they couldn't buy anything with it.
-every day one could watch TV a maximum of 2x. The program included a lesson from the dictator about all the achievements of Romania, news, folk music and a short Russian cartoon for children.

2. Was the Ceaușescu dictatorship discussed in elementary school, high school and university?

At school, no, because it was not an examination subject. The history of Romania was taught only until the end of the 1st World War.
At the University in Cluj only a professor from Munich spoke about the Ceaușescu dictatorship. We former Cluj students informed Mr. Kneifel that a demonstration against „Romanian Corruption", for „Common Sense and Education" will take place in Stuttgart on February 12, 2017. It was a demonstration against the communist Ponto government and for democratic structures in Romania. Mr. Kneifel came to the demonstration and we experienced him as we knew him: rock solidly convinced of democratic principles.

3. How do you and your friends assess Romania's political situation today?

Quite badly. The people have learned nothing in the many years and continue to vote for the „communist" party, which calls itself the Social Democratic Party. For years it lies and deceives the people.
There are also multiple angles and opinions:
- those who emigrated see the situation very seriously and try to open the eyes of the others who stayed at home. But they are criticized and called cowardly people, because they left the country and are „not Romanian patriots".
- Others want to leave the country because they no longer see a future for themselves in Romania.
- others are doing so well in Romania because they have their own business and can get along with any political party that governs the country. They think that this behavior is not optimal, but they think that they can't change anything either. But unfortunately, very many Romanians think that way and that's why nothing changes.

No. 9: Name: Pancika G.
Birthplace: Turda   Place of residence: Oldenburg

1. How did your grandparents (grandma and grandpa) and your parents feel about the years under the Ceaușescu dictatorship?

The properties of the grandparents were expropriated. One because they were Transylvanian-Saxons and a socialist LPG (agricultural production cooperative) was to be established on their land. Half of their garden was also taken away. My great-grandmother's house was given to a Roma family to live in. Our family, my great-grandmother's, was to move into the barn. They couldn't do anything about it and were happy to still be able to stay on the farm.

The other grandparents: Grandpa resisted the expropriation of farmland for collectivization. The property of the family was expropriated and the family was forced to move to the city to work as laborers in the factories. They were very poor and barely had the bare necessities. My great-great-grandfather was one of the few liberal mayors in Romania. This circumstance will also have influenced the harsh expropriation measures. Then followed the forced resettlement in the city.

My parents: My father started working at an early age and attended school in the evenings on the side in order to be able to take his Abitur and study. He became an engineer. My mother became a teacher and, as was customary at the time, taught not only foreign languages but also political education, which was in keeping with the regime of the time. Nevertheless, my parents deliberately stayed away from active politics as best they could.

I am writing this small insight into the family history, which I consider important. I consider an individual confrontation with the Ceaușescu period relevant in order to resolve the traumas inflicted.

My childhood took place in an economically successful larger village, which for centuries was dominated by Saxons, who in turn emigrated, first sporadically and then increasingly after the political change. This mass emigration runs parallel to the processes of coming to terms with communism and is at times emotional. Therefore, the Saxon controversy is always overlaid with these additional incisions. The village landscape was very much changed, as there were many expropriations of the previous generation.

2. Was the Ceaușescu dictatorship discussed in elementary school, high school and university?

I can remember the turnaround very well. I was 6 years old at that time. I can remember the television broadcasts and the execution of Nicolae and Elena Ceaușescu and the alleged course of the revolution. There was little clarity about what actually happened. What was conveyed on television, in my childhood memory, was rather the joy of having overthrown the tyrant. In contrast, very little was reappraised at school or at university.

In the leadership were still the party cadres „of the 2nd rank". The general discourse went in the direction: the Ceaușescu family was to blame, everyone else was a victim.

In the 1990s, there were some films that addressed the issue of torture and murder of political prisoners (e.g. Memorialul Durerii). Scenes of the revolution and the execution of Nicolae and Elena Ceaușescu were repeatedly shown on television. Again and again we hear reports about the collaborators of that time. High-ranking church members were also among them. This was partly a reason why the church was not banned during the dictatorship in Romania. However, there was also a lot of resistance from within the church. Members of the Saxon minority were first seen as fascist enemies under communism. Thus, the Protestant and German congregations were generally considered „Nazi German" and treated accordingly.

Anyone who was 18 years old and German was interned after World War II and deported to Russia. Two of my great aunts were thus imprisoned and deported to Russia to work in the mines. My grandmother was able to escape this situation through personal connections and clever courage and was freed after a few hours – before being deported to Siberia. Her two sisters were deported to the USSR. After the fall of communism in 1989, a very large part of the Saxons emigrated. They were afraid of being exposed again to a regime of Ceaușescu supporters. A reappraisal of that time did not come about. People preferred not to deal with it emotionally. In high school, the subject of communism was dealt with, but rather in a bullet-point manner than in depth. At the university, the topic was hardly taken up, except by a foreign professor. A general reappraisal will probably only take place when the generation involved has passed away. In my opinion, children are the drivers of enlightenment and historical reappraisal. Nevertheless, questions and the active questioning of conditions and living circumstances can often be asked more easily by grandchildren than by one's own children. Many young and qualified Romanians see their future rather in the western world: more economic appreciation and more reliable political structures. There is hardly a family in Romania today that has not „lost" family members to the West as guest workers or de facto emigrants. This grandchild generation, which could drive the argument, is missing from the country. It even seems that a collective cloak of silence still prevails today. Perhaps it is also actively pursued out of the inability to emotionally confront.

Too often, it was a matter of pure survival, of starting over again. The educational norm used to be one of „compliance" rather than critical questioning.

3. How do you and your friends assess Romania's political situation today?

I find the political situation in Romania unstable. I hardly follow the news from there anymore. Many of the bright minds have emigrated and the brain drain continues. Corruption still exists on both a small and large scale. The economy seems to form a parallel society. In the economy, some things work very well, even small and medium-sized enterprises function quite well. However, entrepreneurs often get ahead only through bribery.

EU accession was both a blessing and a curse for the country. The bad: many young people emigrated after joining the EU. The good: freedom of movement, being part of a globalized society, control by the EU institutions, economic integration with the EU, which, however, was also accompanied by great inflation and had other disadvantages. Many have placed their hopes in President Johannis, but he has not been able to achieve as much as hoped. If fundamental reforms do not come, it is rather difficult for the country to move forward in the long term. The Corona crisis was partly handled very well in Romania, but it also further destabilized the country. Many of my friends who still live in Romania are disappointed with the structures, even if they are quite well positioned professionally. Some of the young people have a harder time than before raising a family and being successful professionally. At the same time, however, they feel part of a globalized world and are very well connected internationally: cosmopolitan and adaptable.

Despite the political burden that weighs on Romanians, the country offers many opportunities: Flexibility, cordiality and cohesion. That has not been lost on the people of Romania, and I am very grateful for that. Hardworking and smart people get ahead there, too.

No. 10: Name: Lenya G.
Place of birth: Constanța   Place of residence: Sibiu

1. How did your grandparents (grandma and grandpa) and your parents feel about the years under the Ceaușescu dictatorship?

Such an answer depends on what social and economic situation one found oneself in after the fall of communism. We compared our situation under the communists with the other states in Europe and did not have high expectations either.

My grandfather was urged to join the Romanian Communist Party. Since he managed a hospital, membership in the Communist Party was mandatory. In the 50's and 60's, the academics and the qualified Romanians were not only pushed out by the communists, but also physically removed. My grandfather considered membership in the RKP a formality, which he explained to me several times. He tried to do his work at the hospital correctly under the circumstances.

After the fall of communism, he explained to me that he had probably been under surveillance by the Securitate. The reason: he had accidentally thrown a letter in the trash instead of burning it. According to his feeling, an unofficial employee of the Securitate must have forwarded the letter. As we know today, the Securitate had 85,000 full-time and 800,000 part-time employees who monitored neighbors and friends.

My grandfather also reported that he and the whole family suffered greatly under the communists. Their living conditions were completely turned upside down. Almost all the family property was confiscated, including a water mill that had been in the family for generations. My unforgotten grandfather knew from his childhood what life could be like without a communist regime.

After the fall of communism in 1989, he joined a party that opposed Iliescu and Co. He told me back in 1989 that Iliescu and his friends wanted to continue the communist regime in Romania and had organized Ceaușescu's execution. Few Romanians believed this statement at the time.

My grandfather hoped to help build a Romania with democratic structures in 1989. But his friends were convinced that Ceaușescu's successors would continue to lead Romania forever.

My father often told me what the communists had done to his village in the early 1950s. That is why he did not become a member of the RKP. He deeply rejected party membership out of opportunism. The farmers were deprived of their cows and horses as well as their carts and plows. In the village square they threw down the tools taken from the peasants, which rusted and rotted there.

On my mother's side, the ancestors were teachers, they were not opportunists. I was told a thousand times by my parents the true face of Romania's communists.

In the towns and villages, the acceptance of the communists was different. In the small villages, people tried to get along with the communists as well, while in the cities they avoided them.

2. Was the Ceaușescu dictatorship discussed in elementary school, high school and university?

Since we attended school and university after the fall of communism, it was difficult for us to question our parents' communist period. Some students praised the time under Ceaușescu, others strongly criticized it. We had a German lecturer who described himself as a citizen of the world. He explained to us in a political science lecture the basics of democracy with all its strengths and weaknesses, fascism and communism. This lecture was the reason for me and some other students to study the recent history of Romania. As I heard later, the foreign professor was not allowed to give any more lectures in political science. He was told that only Romanians could properly assess communism in Romania.

In the university, some students said that under communism, food was rationalized and there was a ban on travel abroad.

My wife grew up in a typical gray apartment block in the city. She told me about life in „real" communism. In the apartment blocks cold water was rationalized, it was available only two hours in the evening. Hot water was often not available in apartment blocks, it had to be heated on the stove. People were told that industry needed the water. Since I, unlike my wife, grew up in a small town, we used wood to heat what we could get.

3. How do you and your friends assess Romania's political situation today?

In Romania, it is often said that the communist idea of the parents often lives on in the children. The parents then speak of the so-called „achievements" of communism.

Before the fall of communism in 1989, few could draw a comparison between the economic situation in Romania and that of Western Europe. During communism in the former German Democratic Republic, about 3 million Germans fled to West Germany between 1948 and 1989. If life under communism had been so pleasant, West Germans would have moved to the GDR.

Another comparison: If the Communist idea had worked anywhere in the world, the Swiss and the Scandinavians would have become Communists long ago. The Communist parties in these countries score less than 3% in the elections. It is depressing that the Romanian Communist Party, which calls itself the Social Democratic Party, is the strongest party in Romania. Romania is the only country in Europe that has such a strong communist party.

Democracy as a system is not criticized in Romania, but the approach of Romanian politicians. I often hear that Romanian politicians cannot work together. Everyone wants to be first, everyone wants to be in charge. They have heard nothing about the common good, they just want to line their pockets.

I read that only in Romania do politicians switch from one party to another when they are promised a ministerial post in another party. Romania has had seventeen prime ministers since 1989; Germany has had only four chancellors.

Romania today has some economic regions, so-called clusters, which are comparable to those in Western Europe. They are located in the western part of Romania. When local politicians push the industrialization of their region, tax revenues create opportunities to renovate hospitals, strengthen education and renew roads.

I hear from friends that, unfortunately, Romanian factories had no future after the fall of communism in 1989. Except for agricultural products, Romania had no products that it could have sold on the world market. 90% of the goods produced in Romania went to the Eastern Bloc countries, Korea, Cuba and Vietnam. They were not competitive.

Within the framework of the Moscow Conference of the Allied Great Powers from October 9 to 20, 1944, Churchill and Stalin determined the future spheres of influence in the countries of Southeastern Europe on October 9, 1944. Influence over Romania was left 90% to the Soviet Union and only 10% to Britain and the United States. Influence over Yugoslavia and Hungary was to be split 50%-50% between the Soviet Union and Britain in conjunction with the United States. Churchill felt that Romania was better left in Moscow's sphere of interest because of its history. Stalin, according to Churchill, confirmed the proposal by putting a check mark on the sheet. The U.S. did not sign this document because it did not participate in the October 9-20, 1944 conference in Moscow.

The future of Romania was determined at the Yalta Conference. The protocol of the negotiations at the Crimean Conference on Sunday, February 11, 1945 consists of 14 chapters. In Chapter 11, the future of Romania is determined.

The history of Romania would have been different after 1989 if Mihail I had become the king and president of Romania. Instead, Iliescu and comrades continued to govern Romania along Ceaușescu's lines.

We must not forget that Great Britain and Germany had functioning heavy industry before WW1, while the Czechs, Slovaks and Poles built it up only between WW1 and WW2. Romania and Bulgaria brought up the rear, trying to build heavy industry only after WW2. Romania lost at least 60 years to build an industry due to the Gheorghiu-Dej and Ceaușescu years. It must be possible to sell the products on the world market. The Western European countries do not stop in their development, which we see in the latest climate technology. For the German industry, climate neutrality is to take place by 2030.

New industries are emerging in Western Europe, where computer-controlled wind turbines, solar power plants and off-shore wind farms are being built. Under Ceaușescu, Romania ranked 89th in innovation, just ahead of Burundi. Today, Romania already ranks 50th in the world in innovation, an enormous advance.

Many of my acquaintances claim that Romania's economic and political situation has deteriorated in recent years. However, they do not want to recognize Romania's progress because they expect too much from the local authorities. Romanians are beginning to realize that democracy must be fought for every day. Romania will look different if everyone asks themselves first, „How can I solve my problem?" and not wait for the state. I am responsible for my own life.

Romania has a future only in the EU and NATO. Otherwise, it will fall into the sphere of interest of Russia, China or Turkey. Without the EU and NATO, Romania's fate is sealed. Romania is not economically or militarily viable in a globalized world. Romania's share of world trade is 0.3%.

No. 11: Name: Oana and Amalia C.
Birthplace: Lugoj   Place of residence: Berlin

1. How did your grandparents (grandma and grandpa) and your parents feel about the years under the Ceaușescu dictatorship?

Zero freedom of expression

Pavel, my maternal grandfather, was born in 1922 in Chișinău, now the capital of Moldova. He died in 2011 in Lugoj, a small town in western Romania. My grandfather grew up under the Romanian King Mihai I and never came to terms with the regime change to communism. **Pavel was against the communist regime with his whole being, but he restrained his words out of fear.** After all, he knew what people were capable of because he had served in World War 2 and had witnessed much cruelty first hand. His youngest daughter, Veronica, was my mother. There was little talk at home about the communist dictatorship. Therefore, it is still unclear why the family home was once searched by the Securitate and my grandfather was sent to prison for a few days. It could have been because my grandfather owned books critical of the system that his brother had written. Another possible reason could be that his son, as a young entrepreneur, printed clothes for teenagers.

Monarchy and dictatorship

My grandfather Pavel was one of nine children and came from a family where education was highly valued. Perhaps it is also due to the fact that my great-grandparents had no opportunity for higher education. Among the siblings were writers, mathematicians and lawyers. When the Russians came to Chișinău, the family had to leave everything behind and left for the West by horse-drawn wagon. As a result, the family was scattered to all parts of Romania. My grandfather's siblings, who were „in hiding" at the beginning, nevertheless had an intimate relationship with each other. Less so, however, with the youngest brother, who was the only one who had decided to work „close to the system. But close to the system still did not mean that he joined the

Communist Party. „In our house, no one was in the party!" my mother said proudly. **In my grandfather's eyes, like almost all his siblings and their own families, only uncouth people and without backbone could serve such a system.** In the very close family circle, my grandfather also expressed such views, with quite a bit of irony and disgust. „The more educated a person was, not only in the sense of school education, but in the sense of humanity, the less he could do with state regulations. Then, at work, my father was put in front of such uneducated but line-loyal superiors", my mother explained now.

Religion and contempt for humanity

My grandfather Pavel remains to this day the person with the greatest love of books I have ever known. I am deeply grateful to him that I grew up with ancient Greek legends. I can recognize constellations and know how to lovingly care for nature. My unforgotten grandfather also worked for a time as a forester and rode his horse across Romania for a living. I learned humanity and openness from him. Since my great-grandmother was Jewish, my grandpa never behaved or expressed xenophobic attitudes. He also never spoke negatively against the Roma, which was still common in Romania and unfortunately still is. He also abhorred domestic violence and never beat his wife or my mother. This is a rarity in Romania. My grandfather did not present any religion to me as the right one. He wanted me to be kind-hearted to all the people I dealt with, even if they wanted to harm me, until one might think I was naive. In his view, people thousands of years from now would look at our pompous Orthodox churches, for example, the way we look at the pyramids now in wonder but not in belief. For him, nature was spiritual (and the union between humans and nature was the closest thing to religion). **My grandfather's atheistic worldview seems to coincide with the communist idea. The fundamental difference, however, is that goodness had no place in communism, but it was so central to my grandfather.**

School and media

Because of my grandfather's love of books, my grandmother became a bookseller. She was able to practice this profession when her children were older and she did not yet have to raise grandchildren. Even though my grandmother was rather a quiet person, she was upset about the communist propaganda literature. Books, such as international literature, were almost impossible to acquire. This was only possible secretly through contacts or had to be bought as a bundle together with 3 propaganda books. In the windows of the bookstores, there was always only the book series „Romania on the Road to Socialism". This is where the joke that „Romania is on the road (the road to socialism)" comes from. There was also nothing on TV or in the newspapers except propaganda/news. In our area we could sometimes receive radio broadcasts from Hungary and Serbia. Provided one had electricity, especially since daily power outages were normal. From Munich, one could listen to „Free Europe" – despite the reception interference systems – to find out what was actually going on in one's own country. In order to give the three children better educational opportunities, my grandparents then decided that the children, including my mother, **could attend a school where as little Russian as possible was taught. English, French and German were to broaden the children's horizons.** My grandfather Pavel attended the evening school in the monastery in our hometown of Lugoj in western Romania to learn German.

Career and party affiliation

My mother Veronica became an electrical engineer, my aunt a doctor and my uncle a mechanical engineer. During their studies, students who were in the Communist Party received bonus points. The professors who were less good or less willing to work secured themselves by being in the party. It was a collection of less intelligent and very lazy people. They got a good job through the party without having to work much: For example, they would spend a day at work observing how the water flowed, and then take a sample. **On their own merits, such people**

would not have made it far in life. „But as party members, some could become ministers", my mother explained.
Other ways to get a good job was, for example, in the city administration. There one had a separate access to better food. Another possibility was also to work directly in food sales. There one had access to food and got a lot of bribe money to sell the better food to others. To get this job, one had to pay a large gold coin as a bribe oneself to be hired in the beginning. Everyone else who did not have direct access to food had to stand in line for hours to buy just the bare necessities to survive. „Liver sausage with beard" consisted of hairy pig skin, which was found in all parts of the sausage.

Economy and hunger
Everyday life was hard for most people, especially in the 1980s, when Ceauşescu wanted to pay off all foreign loans early. He stopped imports and there was a shortage of everything. Before the 80s there were sweets, fine meat or good bread to buy, after that everything disappeared. In the 80s, almost all goods were rationed, from milk to textile materials. Everything was available only through ration cards per family member. Some products were no longer available at all, such as oranges or coffee. This was only available with the addition of ground chickpeas. „**On the Romanian market at that time, for every 3 lei (Romanian currency at that time, plural), there was only 1 leu (Romanian currency at that time, singular) of goods. There was nothing to spend your money on. You could only hope to barter with others**", my father told me. Stealing from the workplace for barter was widespread. The motto was „man must be able to live from his work." However, if you didn't know anyone who worked in egg or meat production, you had to starve, raise animals yourself, or stand in line. „**Food, like foreign currencies, was extremely valuable. This is how nouveau riche people like Gigi Becali (now a convicted politician) emerged, who at the time raised sheep near Bucureşti and sold or bartered dairy products at horrendous prices**", my father

explains. „When you saw a line of people in front of a store, you immediately got in line without knowing what was being sold, because there was a shortage of everything", my mother told me. „Usually in the stores there was only toilet paper, canned shrimp or fish, otherwise complete emptiness", my mother recalled. She had to wait in line a lot in the 1980s, including during her two pregnancies. After we were born, other family members stood in line to buy milk for the infants, for example. Our great uncle even lost his life in the process: He left around 3 o'clock in the night to stand in line so that his grandchildren could have milk. It was a very cold winter night and he suffered a heart attack and died there in the line of people.

Housing and living

Even if one could not afford anything from one's money, work was compulsory. „Social parasites" were regularly collected by the militia. After graduation and compulsory military service, which also applied to women, **everyone was assigned a job, far away from home. One was separated from the family, so that one was more dependent on the state.** People from the richer west of the country were often sent to the poorer east. In the Moldova region, not to be confused with the Republic of Moldova, life was very difficult. Railroad trains from the Moldova region were called „hunger trains." People moved away from there to avoid dying there.

Another aspect that made life difficult and cost many women their lives was the illegality of abortions. In addition to the assigned job, there was a prefabricated apartment to the following criteria: Family size, study or grease. On the other hand, if you had a house where you could squeeze in even more people, a tenant was forcibly assigned to the owner. My paternal great-grandfather was the rope maker in his town. The communists took away his business along with the commercial building and land. The former employees, apprentices and master craftsmen had to work in a state enterprise from then on. A normal earning person could not afford a car, like a qualified factory worker, master craftsman, factory director or school teacher. Only people who worked in the state service, that is, where you did not have to do anything, so „la stat se stă". There you could steal or get bribes or both. But even then you had to be on the waiting list for 5 years until you were allowed to buy the car.

Revolution 1989

When the revolution finally began in 1989, my mother Veronica was in Timişoara on business, near the home of László Tökes, an Evangelical Reformed clergyman. He is considered the trigger of the Romanian Revolution. Trains stopped running, they didn't know why. My mother, however, had to go home to her small children and to her friend's newborn. She wanted to sew diapers for her as a present, since her friend had been released from the hospital that very day. As my mother walked for hours through the city towards the train station, at some point she encountered demonstrators and the militia. The militia banged their plastic signs quite loudly and the protesters yelled. „If I don't get through here now, I won't make it home", my mother thought to herself and walked right between the two groups. „Of course I was scared, I didn't know what was happening. The streets were dark, I was alone. It wasn't until late at night that my train left for Lugoj. When I finally got home, I had to talk for hours about what had happened before I could calm down a bit." Our father eventually had to sew the diapers himself.

Only six days later, on December 20, the revolution of Timişoara came also to Lugoj. Timişoara is the first revolutionary city and is 60km away from Lugoj, the second revolutionary city. The communist dictatorship tried with all its might to put down the revolution and to hide everything. Through the radio „Free Europe" we heard that people were fighting for freedom and therefore were shot down by the militia in the streets. At the country level, the revolution was when Ceauşescu was killed on December 22. People shouted in the streets, „Who shot into the crowd on December 22? („cine a tras in noi in 22"). Despite the many deaths, the revolution was also a moment of enormous joy for young and old: „**In a shattered Lugoj, with bullet holes on walls, my grandfather Pavel then crisscrossed the whole city shouting „the pigs are finally gone" (borrowing from Orwell) and crying tears of joy with relief with me, his 2-year-old granddaughter, who was sitting on his bicycle.**

2. Was the Ceaușescu dictatorship discussed in elementary school, high school and university?

No, we didn't talk about the dictatorship in elementary and high school, but our grandparents sometimes talked about it. At that time, our parents had little time to talk about the Ceaușescu period. They worked full time and opened some grocery stores in addition. However, they **took** us on many **trips around Romania. For example, we also went to the memorial of the victims of the communist dictatorship in Sighetu Marmației** . We also visited the opera house in Timișoara . There the bullet holes from 1989 were still visible. Here the militia shot at the civilian population. A German guest lecturer was the only one to mention the Ceaușescu dictatorship in a logistics lecture. As he pointed out, the Ceaușescu politicians of that time now call themselves social democrats, which is wrong. They are the old communists.

3. How do you and your friends assess Romania's political situation today?

When I go to vote in Germany today, my Wahl-O-Mat result always says green and pro-social. Unfortunately, in Romania, on the other hand, things are becoming more and more right-wing and populist. Therefore, I have always participated in the Romanian elections, President, MEPs, no matter where I was in the world or how long the lines were in front of the Romanian embassy. When possible, I was also on demos, for example, against Roșia Montana, mining with cyanide. **Unfortunately, there is hardly any nuanced discourse about a pro-social society in Romania, as the communist dictatorship left**

deep wounds in the collective conscience. The distinction between political and social systems is completely blurred. Democracy is equated with ruthless capitalism. This is a great pity, because the Social Democratic Party in Romania cannot be compared to the social democrats of Western Europe. The communists before 1989, now call themselves social democrats (Partidul Social Democrat, PSD). They act with the same spinelessness as back then and are not electable for me and my immediate acquaintances. **In general, the corruption in Romania – then as now – is enough to make one pull out one's hair, as is the influence of politics on the media and on the beneficial relationship between the Orthodox Church and the state.** Considering these facts, one should not be surprised at so much agitation and hatred. These resentments are directed against poor people, refugees, people from other religious or ethnic backgrounds, and especially against Roma, Jews and people from the LGBTQ community and women. All prejudices are projected onto them. In short, only the white, heterosexual, Christian man is valid.

In this way, people are divided and distracted from corruption and other major problems such as health and education. That's why I also left Romania and don't want to return there.

What still gives me hope are people like Mrs. Kövesi, who fearlessly fights against corruption, or ordinary people on the streets at demos. Only time will tell whether Romania will become 'o țara ca afară' (a country like those outside) after all.

No. 12: Name: Alina D.
Birthplace: Sibiu   Place of residence: Hannover

1. How did your grandparents (grandma and grandpa) and your parents feel about the years under the Ceaușescu dictatorship?

I have access above all to the horizon of experience of my maternal family, with whom I grew up. In addition, my memories are „contaminated" with my own historical „research" and scientific readings. Overall, however, I can say that at the end of the communist era, my entire maternal family found the situation very oppressive – and this despite the fact that my maternal grandfather was a factory party secretary and my parents were both party members. Like many people around us, they played their part in the system. Our mother, because she had to, taught the official world view as a German teacher. At the same time, she could go to church without seeing any real conflict in it. My father was very happy about Ceaușescu's fall and recalled the liberal and conservative traditions in his family that had been brutally suppressed by communism. Because of my mother's Transylvanian-Saxon origins and numerous foreign relatives, we were all very disillusioned anyway about the „Golden Era of Ceaușescu ". Basically, one can say that the victim self-perception predominated in the memory and less the awareness of having been part of the brutal system. What became predominant was the life story, how well one had managed to get by. In comparison, thinking about communism occupies a relatively small place in family memories. For our generation, this reflection is much more intense. For the older family members, the memory of the Russian deportation of many family members after 1944 and the „martyrdom" experienced there dominates. I have not experienced communism nostalgia in anyone in my family environment. It seems to me that communism appears in the family stories as an „unquestioned" fact, as a blueprint for one's own biographical narratives. 1989 was an important turning point.

2. Was the Ceaușescu dictatorship discussed in elementary school, high school and university?

I attended German school in Romania, where in the 1990s surprisingly little was said about the communist period. This has to do with the fact that communism was „exorcised" from the public image. No one wanted to be associated with it. While I was working, the question arose for the first time in my mind as to which people in my environment had previously worked for the Securitate.

In 2004, the Ceaușescu pictures had practically disappeared from the public eye for years and were very hard to find. At that time I found a picture of Ceaușescu and asked my students who this man actually was. I was very surprised when the students asked me whose picture I was holding.

3. How do you and your friends assess Romania's political situation today?

The answer to this question is very complicated. The last few years have been marked by a rapid change from a mood of optimism to one of resignation. The geopolitical climate is pulling developments in the country into new waters. With the election of a president of German origin, Romanian society has demonstrated a European spirit and greatness. At the same time, we are witnessing the tenacious survival of oligarchic structures rooted in communist times. The bourgeois parties and President Johannis have squandered a historic opportunity for lasting change in Romanian society. The rise of AUR, fueled by perceived reservations about the West and by vaccination hysteria, sheds a completely new light on developments – a very worrying one.

No. 13: Name: Reveca O.
Place of birth: Braşov Place of residence: Bucureşti

1. How did your parents (grandma and grandpa) and your parents feel about the years under the Ceauşescu dictatorship.

My grandparents and parents felt that the dictatorship – like a dictatorship – deprived them of freedom, was oppressive and violent, threatening and characterized by poverty.

My paternal grandfather, always felt persecuted and spied upon and as an amateur hunter, he always sought a refuge in nature.
My father is a native Romanian from Braşov – originally his family comes from the Danube region.
Dad hated the regime because he was an artist and loved freedom. That's why we emigrated to Germany in 1989. He is very interested in history and did not think much of the patriarchal Orthodox Church. Therefore, as an intellectual, he always felt oppressed and restricted during the Ceauşescu period.
My mother is a Szekler from Harghita (Szeklerland) and moved to Braşov in her youth. For her, life was much harder under the Ceauşescu dictatorship, as she comes from a rather wealthy Szekler peasant family. Already because of the Hungarian language – language of the minority – her life and that of her family was marked by discrimination, racism and oppression. As an independent, proud farmer, she knew the hard work she had to continue as a dependent factory worker. But that made her very strong inside.
I grew up in my early years with my Hungarian-born grandparents. Until I was four years old, I spoke only Hungarian. Now I still understand some Hungarian, but I can hardly speak it. As a child, I barely knew the Romanian language. Only with my father's relatives I spoke broken Romanian.

My father was in Berlin when the Wall fell on November 9, 1989. My mother and I followed him to Berlin a few months later. Then followed many stations in asylum homes in the greater Berlin-Brandenburg area.
In kindergarten I learned a first language properly for the first time: it was the German language. That's why I was able to teach my parents the German language. After finishing the 9th grade of high school in Berlin, we moved back to Brașov in 2002. Now I had to learn the Romanian language within a year in order not to be left behind. At first, coming from Germany, I found it very difficult to get around, which was a bit problematic.

In Brașov, I attended the German-speaking Honters Gymnasium, which is known for its high standards and cosmopolitanism. After 12th grade, I stayed at home for another year because I was not accepted at Humboldt. I bridged the time by acquiring a driver's license, attending an art school and doing translations.

At the time, my parents ran these underground meetings where they held video nights. So they were part of these hidden cultural protest movements that were everywhere in Eastern Europe. So they tried to have at least a little bit of joy from life.

Overall, everyone in my family felt an extremely strong dislike for the Ceaușescu regime. They lived in poverty and fear.

2. Was the Ceaușescu dictatorship discussed in elementary school, high school and university?

I can't say much about that, since I attended a Romanian school for 3 years and then a German-language high school. However, in Romanian lessons we dealt not only with Morometii and Ion, but also with Cel mai iubit dintre pamanteni and Padurea Spanzuratiilor. Therefore, I would say that early in the school lessons you came in contact with the dictators in Romanian history.

In the German-language Department of History and Philosophy, we studied the history of Europe: Nationalism, Fascism and Communism. We dealt with Marx and other political theorists. I heard from other students that the Ceaușescu dictatorship was covered in some high schools. This depends on the teachers at the schools and the region.

3. How do you and your friends assess Romania's political situation today?

After a transformation process lasting more than 30 years, the Romanian Parliament is the first pluralistic parliament that is not represented by just one or two parties. This pluralism thus leads to more democracy, but unfortunately also to stagnation in Romania.

However, since society is preoccupied with day-to-day survival, there is little time to actively engage with politics. This leads to political passivity and disenchantment with politics among Romanians. A great many educated Romanians leave the country. The reason is the hoped-for higher standard of living, but also the hope for a functioning constitutional state.

Romanian society is unfortunately politically inexperienced and politically illiterate. In addition, there is a sense of hopelessness after the bloody revolution. Even the protests in many cities in Romania against the old communists in the so-called Social Democratic Party ultimately achieved very little.

Conclusion: The political system is unstable and has many democratic deficits. It is a very weak democracy that remains divided between modernity and anti-modernity (economic system vs. church).

No. 14: Name: Manea C.
Place of birth: București   Place of residence: Constanța

1. How did your grandparents (grandma and grandpa) and your parents feel about the years under the Ceaușescu dictatorship?

My parents suffered a lot under the restrictions of the dictatorship. When I became a father myself, I knew how hard it was for my parents. They couldn't talk to us children about the Ceaușescu dictatorship because they were afraid that their children would tell other children. The other children might then tell their parents. Result: a possible arrest of the parents.

Only now, as a father, I understand that my parents could not discuss everything with us children. It must have been very difficult for my parents. Today I talk about everything I think with my children. The thought of not being able to talk to my children out of fear is inconceivable to me today.

My parents were deeply religious. Ceaușescu had also severely restricted the Orthodox Church from proclaiming the faith. My parents suffered greatly from this as well.

2. Was the Ceaușescu dictatorship discussed in elementary school, high school and university?

I started school in 1990. There was talk of the dictatorship and the revolution even then.

When I was in high school, the textbooks told about the Ceaușescu dictatorship and the revolution. But at that time Iliescu was considered the hero of the revolution. Now in 2022 it is slowly changing. Every year the young generation learns a little more about what was going on back then. The truth cannot be suppressed in the long run.

3. How do you and your friends assess Romania's political situation today?

Very bad. And now, after 30 years, we finally had the opportunity to elect a new party. This party managed to be represented in parliament. But the „traditional" parties (all former communists) have now made a monstrous coalition with the only aim to steal a lot of money from the EU reform program!

It may be that President Johannis is the biggest disappointment in these 30 years. I will never forget that my family lost a whole day of vacation in Florida just to be able to vote. Instead of getting to know Miami, Key West or Orlando better, we went to the Romanian Consulate and stood in line there all day to be able to vote for Johannis. Thousands of Romanians were there. Everyone was hopeful and happy that finally, after 30 years, we could get rid of the communists. Unfortunately, that was not the case.

No. 15: Name: Lucian M.
Place of birth: Mediaș   Place of residence: Stockholm

1. How did your grandparents (grandma and grandpa) and your parents feel about the years under the Ceaușescu dictatorship?

My grandfather told me that only characterless and opportunistic people made a career during the Ceaușescu dictatorship.
In 1944, there were only 400-500 communists in Romania. Within a few years, there were millions of Romanians who belonged to the party. The system completely destroyed the independent thinking of Romanians. Other opinions were not welcome, only those of the superior. Up was „bowing low" to rise in the system, while down was kicking. Hundreds of thousands of Romanians have their hands stained with blood, my devout mother said. At some point in their lives, they will have to atone for their misdeeds.

2. Was the Ceaușescu dictatorship discussed in elementary school, high school and university?

In high school in Mediaș, the dictatorship was not talked about. When a colleague wanted to talk about the Ceaușescu period in history class, the teacher kept silent. He was afraid. There are still many older professors with a dark past. They do not want to and cannot deal with the past. In all other states of the former Eastern Bloc, these Ceaușescu supporters would have been chased away long ago. In Romania, they continue to be supported by old Ceaușescu supporters. We students, too, were raised by our parents not to debate, but to follow the teachers' instructions.

3. How do you and your friends assess Romania's political situation today?

I now live in Stockholm with my Polish wife. In 2017, I wanted to vote at the Romanian Embassy in Stockholm, as thousands of Romanians did. The then socialist Ponta government did everything to prevent Romanians from voting. I cannot understand why the European Union did not intervene.

At the beginning of 2020, I went on vacation to Thailand with my parents. My parents wanted to fly back to Europe during our vacation together. The epidemic caused us great concern because all flights to Europe were canceled. Therefore, we went to the Embassy of Romania in Bangkok and asked for consular assistance as Romanian nationals. We were told that this was our problem and no one could help us. A week later we flew back to Europe with Lufthansa. The German government had flown almost 300,000 Germans and Europeans back to Europe, which I will never forget. Next year I will become a Swedish citizen and I no longer value Romanian citizenship.

No. 16: Name: Mirena D.
Place of birth: București   Place of residence: New York

1. How did your grandparents (grandma and grandpa) and your parents feel about the years under the Ceaușescu dictatorship?

My father was very active politically and fought for our freedom, which always involved certain risks. We children were always told that nothing that was said in the house was allowed to get out. That was difficult for us to understand as small children.
I and my family were in București during the revolution. I was 7 years old at the time, but I can remember one moment clearly: my father grabbed his jacket and was about to leave for the demonstration, with a Molotov cocktail in his hand. My mother stopped him at the door and said, „Don't go! You have children and the risk that something will happen and you won't come back is too big! Then my father said: That's exactly why I HAVE to go, BECAUSE I have children!
He came back and then we emigrated to Germany, in a Trabi and started everything anew. My parents were already 50 years old. In Germany we were considered foreigners and treated accordingly. My parents could not work as engineers, but what is freedom worth to you? My parents never regretted anything and in our house we talked a lot and about everything. My parents always taught me that there are no good or bad choices, only choices! I think that's why it was easy for me to move around the world three times with toddlers. My parents are almost 80 years old and live in Romania. They are lively and full of zest for life.
My grandmother was a history teacher and was deeply affected by the Ceaușescu dictatorship. She often spoke of the maltreated country that was taken away from her by the communists. My other grandma was often in Germany on „business trips" because she spoke fluent German. We as children always thought this was great, as we had toys that no one else had. What was behind her „business trips" is debatable.... I

never got to know my grandpas, I was a „late child". Overall, however, the mood in my family was: as decent and educated people, you cannot and will not support Ceaușescu and communism.

I have often heard these sayings, nowadays in 2022, that it was better back then because you didn't have to worry about anything. But never in my family. I think these are the people who are afraid of change, because change is hard and tedious. But only change brings people forward. These people are not change agents, not visionaries. But they are the ones who criticize the change-makers, the visionaries, first.

2. Was the Ceaușescu dictatorship discussed in elementary school, high school and university?

At school, there wasn't much talk about the Wende in 1989. Maybe I can't really talk about it because we moved to Germany after the Wende. In Germany, I went to elementary school.

I then graduated from Brukenthal High School in Sibiu. There was not much politicking. The mood at Brukenthal Gymnasium was similar to that in my family. Communism and Ceaușescu dictatorship: no, thanks!

At university, I actually had little contact with the subject. Perhaps also because I shied away from the subject and always tried to run away from it. What did not pass me by, of course, were those Romanian professors who could not or would not free themselves from their past. I avoided these professors quite successfully wherever I could. After all, I wanted to look forward to the future.

When my husband and I had the opportunity to emigrate to America, we never looked back. I worked very hard and determinedly for it.

3. How do you and your friends assess Romania's political situation today?

Especially the people who spent several years in the Ceaușescu dictatorship, my parents' age, asked us why we wanted to emigrate. After all, we had everything we needed in Romania. That's not so wrong, we didn't miss much. However, we were missing something: opportunities for development, recognition, freedom, political stability and a salary according to Western standards, so that we could travel!

A future for us and our children means living a self-determined life.

I do not judge the people who ask us these questions. After all, they don't know anything else, they live in their own world in Romania. I think that the dictatorship would have been less „successful" if people had been able to travel. But traveling broadens the horizon, and that's what the Romanian Communist Party didn't want, because the people were to be lied to and manipulated.

I don't have very much to say about Romania's political situation today, because I inwardly distance myself from it by my own choice. I think that one, two or three? generations are necessary to bring about a change in Romania. My friends and acquaintances who still live in Romania complain the most that nothing will ever change in Romania. I believe that you have to change yourself first. Many forget that a country/state is the reflection of its inhabitants. The government elected in Romania was elected by Romanians. It is the reflection of society.

My family (husband and two children) live a happy, self-determined life in the USA. The USA offers a lot of opportunities to people like us. The difference with Europe is that if you work hard, it is recognized. You are responsible for yourself. I feel like I have my life in my own hands.

6 years ago we bought a family house and also a caravan with which we are „on the road" during the vacations. Now we have bought another small cottage directly on a lake, where we spend the weekends. Of course we have two cars to be independent.

This year we visited Sibiu, where my parents live. It was all beautiful, but we have also become different people through our years abroad. That is why we will not return to Romania. Now our parents are visiting us in New York State.

No. 17: Name: Vladiana A.
Place of birth: Galați   Residence: Dubai

1. **How did your grandparents (grandma and grandpa) and your parents feel about the years under the Ceaușescu dictatorship?**

As my grandparents and parents told me, the teachers were enthusiastic supporters of Ceaușescu. Only those who were loyal to the system could become teachers. Romanians of Hungarian descent were not allowed to teach geography and/or history. Thus, they would have had to teach about the Treaty of Trianon (June 4, 1920) and the Second Vienna Arbitration Award (August 30, 1940).

My grandmother told of the „pioneer commander" of the class, whose job was to write reports about her classmates. My grandmother spoke of a teacher she remembered well. The teacher, Felicia, was a self-assured pioneer leader at school whom most of the students despised. She wanted to manipulate our thoughts and actions. At the school entrance she checked the uniforms with the matriculation number on the sleeve. The husband of the teacher Felicia was a part-time employee of the Securitate, as were another 800,000 Romanians.

In winter, we students froze in unheated classrooms.

After graduating from high school, one could not study whatever one wanted. The decisive factors were the parental home and proximity to the Ceaușescu system.

My grandparents, who were Banater Swabians, suffered under the system. In 1988 they were „ransomed" by the Federal Republic of Germany. Ceaușescu had sold members of the German minority to the Federal Republic of Germany for 2 billion DM. Likewise, Honecker had also sold GDR dissidents to the Federal Republic of Germany.

2. Was the Ceauşescu dictatorship discussed in elementary school, high school and university?

At the university, a German professor taught the subject of political science. He explained the differences between democracy, communism and fascism.

3. How do you and your friends assess Romania's political situation today?

Those students who studied or worked abroad want to leave Romania. But there are also students whose grandparents/parents benefited greatly during the Ceauşescu period. After Ceauşescu's death, these families were suddenly democrats. They are opportunists, just like many in this country.
I worked at Tarom in Bucureşti for a few months: total confusion, no functioning management. In its entire history, Tarom never had a balanced business result, only a negative balance. The so-called senior managers were mostly relatives of politicians from all parties. I had a chance to move to Emirates in Dubai. Tens of thousands of Romanians work in the Emirates. The Emirates airline provided training. The capable employees receive a contract and earn 5 times as much as at Tarom. Romanians should be aware that many things the state does not work. Nobody feels responsible.
Since Romanian state employees have to fly on Tarom for official flights, Tarom flights to Bucureşti are at capacity. Since the airline always makes losses, for the last 30 years it has been said: We make a restructuring of Tarom and demand and receive money from the EU. The EU pays and after a year the process is repeated. Then an experienced foreign manager is hired as CEO, who is immediately opposed by the old clan. Instead of hiring 50 or 60 foreign managers with many years of management experience at Tarom, only one manager is hired as a token. After a few weeks/months, the foreign manager resigns as CEO because the Romanian department heads fight him, especially

since changes mean a threat to their own position. The situation is similar in many Romanian state-owned enterprises.

Perhaps Emirates should take over the management of Tarom for two to five years. All incompetent Romanian employees should be fired and the remaining employees should be subjected to training. But since nothing will change, Tarom ranks 124th in the World Wide Ranking.

Not a single pilot at Tarom has a license for long-haul flights, as Tarom only flies short- and medium-haul routes. Tarom's hangar in Bucureşti houses two new long-haul aircraft that Prime Minister Ponta ordered in 2013. They were not paid for by the airline but by the state, which does not comply with EU directives. When Tarom wanted to check whether these two new aircraft were still operational, no Tarom employee with a long-haul license could be found. For this reason, Air-France was asked to have some pilots perform long-haul flights with the aircraft, which had not been used for years, to determine their technical condition. Romania had paid 800 million euros for the two aircraft, today they are worth about 60-80 million. Of course, no one was responsible.
Result: Nothing will change either.

No. 18: Name: Liana G.
Birthplace: Craiova   Place of residence: București

1. How did your grandparents (grandma and grandpa) and your parents feel about the years under the Ceaușescu dictatorship?

My grandparents had experienced the 1st and the 2nd World War. Especially the family on my mother's side had to suffer. They were decent, hardworking people. My grandfather had built the family house and barn himself. He was a genius because he could manage the big farm well. He could work wood, sole shoes, and grow grapes. He also kept horses, cows and poultry. The family had many children who had to help in farming after school. A mayor was also from our family. My grandmother's brother became a priest and was imprisoned during the Ceaușescu dictatorship.

The grandparents wanted to stay on the farm in the village because they did not want to leave the property of their ancestors. They were called boyars (large landowners) and had to pay high taxes. If they could not pay the taxes, the animals were confiscated. It is strange that the people living in the city looked down on the peasants in the village. Many of the traditions could not be continued and thus knowledge accumulated from generation to generation was lost in experience.

The destruction of farms deepened the identity and knowledge gap in the countryside. Neighborly togetherness was gradually destroyed and the scale of values turned upside down.

The farmers were promised equality in 1946: Everyone 2 goats, even the neighbor should own 2 and not 3 goats. The reality was different. Terrible poverty for everyone, except for the communist elite. There was little talk about the deportations from the Bărăgan or the communist prisons in Pitești, Gherla, Sighet or Aiud. Innocent people were murdered there: priests, teachers, writers, peasants and historians.

The communists not only destroyed the structure of the villages by collectivizing the land, but they forcibly evicted the peasants into poor rented apartments in prefabricated buildings in the cities. These had thin walls, small rooms made of concrete, and were cold. Electricity and water were rationalized. This forced industrialization in Romania had no connection to reality: raw materials, location, costs and efficiency were not taken into account. The construction of hydroelectric plants, irrigation systems and the building of roads were financed by the World Bank.

The decent leaders who wanted nothing to do with communism were replaced by communists. Now the new communist leaders, including civil servants, could abuse their office for corruption.

2. Was the Ceaușescu dictatorship discussed in elementary school, high school and university?

Very little was said in school about the Ceaușescu regime. There were still old history books in which the megalomania of the dictator was evident.

Before the elections, some political parties discussed the advantages and disadvantages of communism. Some documentaries about the Ceaușescu period were also broadcast on television.

I visited the Sighet Memorial as a student to understand the horrors of that time. Now more and more students are writing their doctoral thesis on the crimes of the communist system. At some Romanian universities this is possible, but only with the younger professors who are unencumbered.

3. How do you and your friends assess Romania's political situation today?

Romania's political crisis, which has been going on for years, is based on decisions made by politicians who have no expertise and are completely incompetent.

If young people dare to become active in political parties at the local or national level, they fail because of the established structures of the parties that control the media. Small changes in the balance of power take place only within the relatively small party spectrum. The political parties do everything they can to remain in power over the long term. Party ideologies are interchangeable. The only thing that counts in the political networks are personal, often kinship relationships, which are characterized by opportunism and nepotism.

If you analyze the vitae of politicians, you find that they are mostly uneducated. That is why the young Romanians resign themselves to taking on any responsibility at all in a political party.

No. 19 Name: Anda D.
Birthplace: Sibiu   Place of residence: Sibiu

1. How did your grandparents (grandma and grandpa) and your parents feel about the years under the Ceaușescu dictatorship?

It was a difficult time. But it was better and more beautiful than it is today. Back then, all people were equal, which is not the case today. In the past, you practiced your profession until you retired. Today you can lose your job, which is not good. When you got sick, you went to the hospital and didn't have to worry about getting paid. Today, you have to bribe the doctors and nurses to get treated. This was not the case during the Ceaușescu period.

2. Was the Ceaușescu dictatorship discussed in elementary school, high school and university?

The Ceaușescu period was hardly talked about. Neither at high school nor at university. Even today I am afraid to express my opinion freely, which my parents had advised me to do. They also forbade me to participate in demonstrations. They said that maybe a new socialist government will come when Europe and the USA are no longer interested in Romania. My father believes that the Russians and Chinese want to incorporate Romania, Bulgaria, North Macedonia, Montenegro, Serbia, Bosnia-Herzegovina and Albania into their sphere of power.

3. How do you and your friends assess Romania's political situation today?

The democracy that works in Western Europe cannot function in Romania. Here, the decisions are made by mafia-like businessmen with the politicians of the various parties. The so-called free elections are only used to get money from the European Union. The smart students and flexible students who attended high school and university with me have long since left the country. I do not know anyone who returned from abroad. I also want to emigrate to Australia, where a friend of mine is married and became happy.

In dictatorships, most people are followers. They don't want to know about the crimes, about the concentration camps. This was the case in Nazi Germany, in the GDR, in Russia and in Romania. Most people tacitly accepted the crimes in order to gain advantages (better housing, better jobs, a better place to study, etc.). After the end of the dictatorship in 1989/1990, very many people lacked the courage to make a new start in a democracy they could do nothing with. A civil society could not emerge in Romania, because the henchmen of the Securitate were everywhere. It is supposed to take several generations until democratic structures are eventually established in Romania. That, too, is uncertain.

No. 20 Name: Petre Z.
Place of birth: Bistrița   Place of residence: Vancouver

1. How did your grandparents (grandma and grandpa) and your parents feel about the years under the Ceaușescu dictatorship?

Difficult, but bearable! My grandparents and also my parents had no initiative. They lived in constant anxiety and fear all their lives. Ceaușescu referred to the Romanians as „corn pudding" that would not explode. My parents went to Vienna for a few days in 1990 and were amazed at life in a free society. But they had no initiative and were content to do a job at the post office for life. They were always afraid of losing the job at the post office.

I asked my parents how it was even possible to have two million Romanians arrested by Romanians during the Ceaușescu dictatorship. Their explanation: they were defamed by relatives and neighbors for having made anti-government statements. For such a statement they received various privileges from the Securitate. Nowhere in Europe, except in the Soviet Union, has there been such a brutal system, where prisoners in the Pitești concentration camp had to torture each other under supervision.

2. Was the Ceaușescu dictatorship discussed in elementary school, high school and university?

Only at high school and university was the subject touched upon. I always had the feeling that teachers were very afraid to talk about politics. For them it was important to maintain a secure salary and „status": whether in Ceaușescu, in the current so-called Romanian democracy, or in a possible renewed dictatorship in Romania, which I believe is possible. The teachers/professors were the biggest supporters of Ceaușescu, my grandparents said. Whether this is true, I cannot say.

3. How do you and your friends assess Romania's political situation today?

Hopeless and without a future! My grandparents and my mother have passed away. My brother has been living in Canada for 12 years. That is why I emigrated to Canada, to live my life on my own terms. It is unlikely that I will return to Romania. Here in Vancouver I enjoy the freedom.

No. 21 Name: Viorica M.
Place of birth: Cluj-Napoca   Place of residence: Cluj-Napoca

1. How did your grandparents (grandma and grandpa) and your parents feel about the years under the Ceaușescu dictatorship?

They felt financially secure because they were allotted an apartment and had jobs. Unfortunately, there was very little to buy for the money. My grandparents and parents felt safe because the CPR took care of them and they only had to follow the instructions, which did not bother them. The rationalization of food was also bearable for them.

2. Was the Ceaușescu dictatorship discussed in elementary school, high school and university?

Yes, but only very superficially. Many older teachers did not want to deal with their own past during the Ceaușescu dictatorship. They feel innocent, although they were a willing „cog" in the system.

3. How do you and your friends assess Romania's political situation today?

I cannot imagine a career with a political party. The political system is corrupt. Corruption and nepotism are widespread at all levels in Romania. The capable students do not want to join any party and do not want to stay in Romania. Romania's problems unfortunately persist – even since the end of the Ceaușescu dictatorship. It was followed by sham democratic governments characterized by corruption and nepotism. I see no way out of this vicious circle. Some serious and competent politicians failed because of the conflicts of interest and resigned. Political education is not promoted in schools and at the university. The devastating consequences are visible.

No. 22 Name: Cosmin S.
Birthplace: Sibiu   Place of residence: Galați

1. How did your grandparents (grandma and grandpa) and your parents feel about the years under the Ceaușescu dictatorship?

Although my grandparents had many limitations back then, they always said that it was better before. My parents are of the same opinion. Times were hard, but no one was „put aside." The social differences were not obvious.

2. Was the Ceaușescu dictatorship discussed in elementary school, high school and university?

Yes, the dictatorship was mentioned in high school.

3. How do you and your friends assess Romania's political situation today?

We no longer trust the current politicians. Most politicians do not seem competent to take care of the welfare of citizens. An example is the pandemic management: after 2.5 years of online studies, the Minister of Education decided that students should return to university lecture halls. The order was issued without justification.

No. 23. Name: Alexandru P.
Birthplace: Craiova   Place of residence: New York

1. How did your grandparents (grandma and grandpa) and your parents feel about the years under the Ceaușescu dictatorship?

For my parents and grandparents, those were the hardest times of their lives: no freedom of expression, no food, only the glorification of Ceaușescu and his regime.

2. Was the Ceaușescu dictatorship discussed in elementary school, high school and university?

Hardly, it was only touched on in passing. A Swiss visiting professor told us the following: After the end of communism in the GDR, all communist state enterprises, universities and hospitals were managed across the board by about 30,000 West Germans with professional experience. During the communist period, management positions were decided not by ability but by party affiliation. Thus, people in the GDR were able to free themselves from the communists within a short time. The professor said that this should have happened in Romania as well: Qualified Austrians, Swiss, Scandinavians, etc. should have taken over the responsibilities and the decisions in Romania after the end of the Ceaușescu dictatorship, which unfortunately was not the case. Ceaușescu's supporters did not want to give up power under any circumstances. When they were economically at the end, they asked for membership in the EU, although Romania did not meet the requirements to join at all and still does not. It was a political decision of the USA. First membership in NATO, then in the EU. Because Romania has a Black Sea coast, it has a geostrategic importance for the USA. I read that former German Chancellor Helmut Schmidt called Romania and Bulgaria's membership a big mistake. Helmut Schmidt mentioned the corruption and the non-functioning legal system, which only follows the political instructions of the party that is in power at the moment.

3. How do you and your friends assess Romania's political situation today?

The DNA of the old Ceaușescu clique has often been adopted by their children and grandchildren. They are only interested in maintaining power and their position, not in the country. Since I do not believe in the future in Romania, I will leave the country shortly for New York. There, after all, there should be one of Romania's many cultural institutes abroad. Switzerland, the Netherlands and the Japanese have no need to maintain cultural institutes abroad – only Romania. The megalomania of Nicolae and Elena Ceaușescu lives on.

No. 24:   Name: Mirela R.
Birthplace: Satu Mare   Place of residence: Buzău

1. How did your grandparents (grandma and grandpa) and your parents feel about the years under the Ceauşescu dictatorship?

Those were very difficult years. My grandparents had a car, which meant a lot at that time. My grandparents and also my parents never dared to speak their mind. They followed the orders of their superiors. As my grandfather told me, the leading positions in all state enterprises and also hospitals, schools and universities were filled by Securitate people. It was not about qualifications, it was about „love" for Ceauşescu . The Romanian people were thrilled that Ceauşescu made almost 200 state visits abroad. Only under him was Romania a recognized power, which is no longer the case today.

2. Was the Ceauşescu dictatorship discussed in elementary school, high school and university?

Yes, but little. We must not forget that at the Academy of Sciences in Bucureşti Elena Ceauşescu was elected president by recognized professors, although she could hardly read and write. Why did the „intellectuals" behave this way? They were interested in their own position. This is how the system operated: prison for the dissenters and power (position and money) for the opportunists. The opportunists had and still have Romania in their grip.

In high school, we were taught by a teacher that Romania is one of the great cultural nations of the world. He referred to young Romanians who wanted to go abroad to study or work as „unpatriotic" Romanians. It was only many years later that I realized that the teacher was very limited in his way of thinking. Unfortunately, this way of thinking still prevails in large parts of Romanian society. The teacher spoke only Romanian and had never been abroad. If he were to visit abroad, his thought pattern would collapse. How can such simple-minded people be employed at school?

3. How do you and your friends assess Romania's political situation today?

I find Romania's current political situation problematic.
The standard of living in Romania was higher than that in Spain and Portugal until World War 2.
I have never understood why Romania has more embassies and consular representations than Switzerland or Norway in all parts of the world. Romania also has many cultural institutes around the world that other countries cannot afford (for example, Switzerland, Sweden or Norway).

The constant reminders from Brussels are necessary, otherwise the political clans would exercise even more power. Romania is now a member of the EU and NATO: economic and military security.
According to President Johannis, Romania feels that it is a second-class NATO state because it is allegedly not sufficiently supported by NATO. Now NATO also sent Portuguese and Belgian soldiers to Romania to support the Romanian army in case of a warlike threat.

I therefore compared Romanian military spending with that of the United States and Germany.

U.S. military spending: 811 billion euros, 3.57% of GDP.
German military spending: 53.2 billion euros, 1.5% of GDP.
Romanian military expenditure: 5.75 billion euros, 2.3% of GDP.
The U.S. spends 71 times as much as Romania on the military, while the Germans spend 10 times as much as the Romanians.
Currently, the U.S. contributes 50% of total NATO spending, while the remaining 50% is borne by NATO's 28 member nations.

No. 25: Name: Lacrima M.
Place of birth: București   Place of residence: București

1. How did your grandparents (grandma and grandpa) and your parents feel about the years under the Ceaușescu dictatorship?

My grandfather and mother have already passed away. They told me when I was a child that the stores were empty. They had to learn to do everything themselves at home. My grandmother made soap by herself. There was little fabric to sew clothes. In winter, my mother wore only a thin jacket to go to school. My mother watched some foreign films during the Ceaușescu years, which were banned in Romania at the time. I owe my preference for classical films to my mother's suggestion.

2. Was the Ceaușescu dictatorship discussed in elementary school, high school and university?

Unfortunately, it was almost not talked about at all. I was personally interested in the Ceaușescu period. At school it was a taboo subject.

3. How do you and your friends assess Romania's political situation today?

If you ask someone in Romania about today's political situation, you will hardly get a satisfactory answer. My friends are very dissatisfied with today's political situation. They criticize the political conditions instead of getting involved in civil society.

In Romanian schools we were not educated to be independent thinkers. The teachers expected cadaver obedience and did not want to hear any other opinion. At the university, we humped low and kicked down in front of the rector and the dean. This is the Romanian concept of moving up the career ladder. That is why I left Romania 12 years ago and will only visit the country while my parents are still alive.

As I have gathered from the media, Romanians expect not only financial benefits from abroad, but foreign aid in case of forest fires in the Carpathians, epidemics, etc....

Foreign countries seem to be responsible for this. Romanian hospitals were unable to care for their own sick during the pandemic. Of course, foreign countries were to blame, especially since Romanian doctors emigrated. The nationalists from the AUR and the supporters of the PSD would be incapable of running a state at all. They want to distract from their inability through their constant criticism.

What am I wondering about?

Romania has about 68,000 soldiers and prefers to rely on NATO instead of itself. What about Finland, for example? Finland, with a population of 5.5 million, maintains armed forces of about 25,000 soldiers. In the event of war, 500,000 men and women who had undergone basic military training can be called to arms. Finland also had great financial difficulties. The country borrowed money from the World Bank, which was repaid. The Finns are too proud a people to demand financial benefits from abroad. The Romanians' way of thinking is unfortunately different.

No. 26: Name: Eleana T.
Birthplace: Arad   Place of residence: Braşov

1. How did your grandparents (grandma and grandpa) and your parents feel about the years under the Ceauşescu dictatorship?

During the communist period, ration cards were allocated and food was rationed. Every Romanian received a quarter of a loaf of bread a day and meat was available only at Easter, Christmas and the first of May. Oranges or bananas were only available at Christmas. The main content of their lives was work. Young people did „compulsory patriotic work" until the age of 25. My grandparents told me the following: The neighborhood children met in an apartment to watch television. The program was short and there were only 2 TV channels. The teachers were brutal. If the students did not obey, they were pushed against the blackboard with their heads. Often the students were beaten with a stick until their hands were swollen. If the students walked through the hallways in the school, which was forbidden, they were pulled by the hair.

2. Was the Ceauşescu dictatorship discussed in elementary school, high school and university?

In the lyceum we had the history of communism as an elective. We watched videos about the festivals and events of that time. This gave us an impression of how our grandparents and parents had lived in the Ceauşescu period.

3. How do you and your friends assess Romania's political situation today?

The political parties do not pursue a clear line. Only empty phrases are produced. Many young Romanians are therefore leaving the country. Political instability is evident in all areas of life. That is why Romania has already had 15 prime ministers since 1989. Romania should take the Scandinavian countries or the Netherlands as a model. There, politicians do not leave a political party so that they can become ministers in another party. They are opportunists. But the parliament is the „reflection of a people", as they say.

No. 27: Name: Anca C.
Birthplace: Vaslui   Place of residence: Bucureşti

1. How did your grandparents (grandma and grandpa) and your parents feel about the years under the Ceauşescu dictatorship?

Unfortunately, I did not get to talk much with my grandparents because they were already very old and showed little interest in talking about the Ceauşescu period. They said that the Ceauşescu period had advantages in terms of a job and an apartment. This was guaranteed by the regime. They did not want change and did not understand why there were different political parties. They preferred a leader who makes decisions and takes care of them.

In the USA, about 4 million people leave their jobs every month to start something new. This does not correspond to the Romanian mentality, especially that of the older population.

2. Was the Ceauşescu dictatorship discussed in elementary school, high school and university?

Yes, this era was mentioned.

3. How do you and your friends assess Romania's political situation today?

My friends and I believe that the political situation in Romania can only be improved by politicians with higher levels of education and „nobler values" (less corruption).

Neither I nor my friends are satisfied with Romanian politics. But a Western democracy cannot and will not work in Romania, because the mindset is different from that in Western Europe.

Most Romanians expect the EU to continue to support Romania financially. Also, unlike Ukrainians, most Romanians would not want to defend the country against foreign aggressors. I don't know any of my friends who would want to defend Romania in case of war. Others are also responsible for defense: NATO and foreign soldiers.

No. 28: Name: Sorana L.
Place of birth: Târgu Mureș   Place of residence: Cluj-Napoca

1. How did your grandparents (grandma and grandpa) and your parents feel about the years under the Ceaușescu dictatorship?

The years under the Ceaușescu dictatorship were very difficult for my grandparents and parents. However, they had everything they needed to live. They told me that the state monitored everything. The Securitate reported on every inhabitant. They would not like to relive the Ceaușescu period, although some things were easier and calmer.

2. Was the Ceaușescu dictatorship discussed in elementary school, high school and university?

It was a big topic at our high school. Communism was discussed in detail. The horrors of the Ceaușescu dictatorship were discussed in detail so that we would not have to experience a dictatorship again. As I heard from other colleagues, communism was not discussed at their high school. It always depends on the teacher.
It was a taboo subject at the university. All discussions were stopped.

3. How do you and your friends assess Romania's political situation today?

After 1989, Iliescu was the so-called savior of Romania. He assured the communists and Securitate people not to allow any legal proceedings against them. He was re-elected 2x because Romanians considered him a role model. The transformation process was slow because people did not want major social changes. Interest in elections is low because most Romanians have no concept of democratic values. They want a president who will take care of them.

No. 29: Name: Felicia F.
Birthplace: Baia Mare Place of residence: Frankfurt (Main)

1. how did your grandparents (grandma and grandpa) and your parents feel about the years under the Ceaușescu dictatorship?

The grandparents had different opinions about life in the Ceaușescu period. They had housing and work, which gave them financial security. They also claimed that industry was developed during the Ceaușescu period. My grandparents complained about the lack of freedom of expression. They could not necessarily trust their friends and acquaintances either, since the Securitate monitored people's lives.

My parents lived under communism for only a short time. They felt finally liberated after 1989, but are still waiting for a functioning democracy. That is, a radical change in the current political system.

2. Was the Ceaușescu dictatorship discussed in elementary school, high school and university?

Very little! But there were also teachers at high school and university who described the Ceaușescu years as good years: everyone had their place in society, there was order and discipline.

3. How do you and your friends assess Romania's political situation today?

Romanians believe that they are not properly represented and that corruption is omnipresent. Typical statement: we are deceived and cheated.
Therefore, it will take several more generations for a „Romanian civil society" to possibly develop. Doubts are warranted, since the Romanian nationalists have a large following. At a meeting in Moldova, Simion (AUR) met with the patriarch of the Romanian Orthodox Church and the president of the Romanian Academy of Sciences. The AUR represents the interests of Romanian nationalists and feels deep ties to Russia.

No. 30:   Name: Viorica P.
Place of birth: Buzău   Place of residence: Graz

1. How did your grandparents (grandma and grandpa) and your parents feel about the years under the Ceaușescu dictatorship?

My grandparents experienced terrible things. They wanted to leave the country and were arrested at the Timiș River on the Serbian border. They were sentenced to 5-year imprisonment and had to suffer in different prisons for more than 3 years. Before they were released, they had to sign a statement that they would never be allowed to talk about their detention. They were broken people at the age of 40. On January 12, 1981, they hanged themselves together. My parents didn't tell me the circumstances of the death until I was an adult. My father married a half-Jewish woman, my mother. Their grandparents were all murdered by the Iron Guard (under Ion Antonescu). The Iron Guard had murdered about 200,000 Jews.

2. Was the Ceaușescu dictatorship discussed in elementary school, high school and university?

Almost not. I couldn't talk about it because otherwise I would have become depressed. I already studied in Graz for a year and have since moved there.

3) How do you and your friends assess Romania's political situation today?

I have been living in Austria for 10 years now and only go back to my country of birth to visit my parents. As I noted, I talked about it with my old schoolmates, because we have different experiences and interests.
Here in Austria, people talk about Nazi crimes and face up to their past. The memorial in Mauthausen, where about 90,000 prisoners died, is

visited by school and university groups. This is also true in Germany, where the extermination of the Jews is part of the curriculum in high schools. In Germany, people face the darkest past of German history, while in Romania they do not want to deal with it.

The Argentine military dictatorship lasted from 1976 to 1983. President Raul Alfonsin, elected in 1983, wanted to achieve a thorough reappraisal of the dictatorship's crimes. Due to massive pressure from the military, the reappraisal was stopped and only resumed in 2003 under President Nestor Kirchner. The military junta was held responsible for the deaths of 30,000 people. Generals Jorge Videla and Emilio Massera were sentenced to life in prison.

What a difference to Romania, the most brutal dictatorship in Europe outside the USSR after World War II! Approx. 100,000 innocent people found death in approx. 100 prisons and approx. 100 execution sites. 2 million members of the Romanian Communist Party and the Securitate bear the responsibility for this, as is also evident from reports of the European Court of Justice. Many members of the Communist Party were members of the party out of conviction, under political pressure or out of pure egoism, in order to gain advantages. The names of the full-time and part-time members of the Securitate and also of the Romanian Communist Party are available today in research sites on communism in the United States (UC Berkeley, Stanford). The Romanian grandchild generation now has the opportunity to get a new picture about their parents or grandparents.

I have never heard of a school or university class visiting Sighet. The reason seems to be that the teachers/profes sors do not want to deal with their involvement in the dictatorship. The young teachers/professors do not yet see their time to change this. They often think of their own careers and do not want to jeopardize them because they fear reprisals from superiors.

I have often wondered why Romania, unlike Poland, the Czech Republic and Hungary, does not have the best status in Western Europe. In

2004, Romania became a member of NATO because the USA has strategic interests in the Black Sea. In 2007 Romania became a member of the EU without meeting the requirements.

Again and again I am surprised about the knowledge of history of my Austrian colleagues. During the Ceaușescu period, about 100,000 Romanian prisoners were murdered by Romanians (Securitate). During the revolution, 1,165 Romanians demonstrating for freedom were shot in 1989/1990. The cases against those responsible were dropped. Today, they receive a high state pension. Meanwhile, I believe that educated foreigners know more about Romanian history than many uneducated Romanians.

The European Court of Justice, at the request of the European Parliament, is dealing with the crimes committed by Romanians against Romanians.

I read German newspapers like FAZ and Spiegel Online every day. The arguments of the Romanian politicians are on a very low level. Unfortunately, corruption is widespread and you can also buy a driver's license for 400 to 500 euros.

Romanians believe that the EU must continue to provide for them financially in the future. They always transfer responsibility to others. The „strong man" is sought to provide for them. Since the end of the Ceaușescu dictatorship 32 years ago, with all the crimes, 25 to 30% of the population still believe that Ceaușescu was a good president.

I wouldn't want to live in a country like that.

No. 31: Name: Vasilica T.
Place of birth: Hunedoara   Residence: Vienna

1. How did your grandparents (grandma and grandpa) and your parents feel about the years under the Ceaușescu dictatorship?

My grandparents and also parents spoke very little about that time. They led a typical Romanian married life. The man decides and the woman has to follow, she is not allowed to contradict or have a different opinion. Especially in families with little education, the man wants to be the macho, although the woman is superior to him in intelligence. She is just not allowed to show it. The children are brought up to be obedient. This is the way it is practiced in society: Family is above everything, men and women who are not married are looked at askance.

Since the political parties also want to retain influence over the Romanians through the Orthodox Church, Orthodox churches continue to be built instead of rental apartments.

2. Was the Ceaușescu dictatorship discussed in elementary school, high school and university?

At school and university, politics was hardly ever discussed. You never knew which side your colleague was on. The teachers/professors always wanted to be on the right side when the political situation changed.

How did Romania behave in World War I and World War II? In 1914, Europe was divided into two blocs. The Central Powers with Germany, Austria-Hungary, Turkey, Bulgaria and Italy were on one side, and the „Entente" with France, Great Britain and Russia on the other. In December 1917, after the withdrawal of the ally Russia, Romania was forced to an armistice and in May 1918 to peace. When the defeat of the German Empire on the fronts became apparent, Romania entered the war again in November 1918 in order to secure Transylvania. Hungary signed the Treaty of Trianon on June 4, 1920, in contradiction: two thirds of its territory fell to the neighboring states, especially to Romania. Now Transylvania also became part of Romania. Romania also received territories inhabited by a majority of Hungarians, such as Szeklerland and numerous areas in the north and northeast.

On November 23, 1940, Romania entered World War 2 on the side of the Axis powers. In Romania's war together with Nazi Germany, 475,000 Romanians died.

On August 23, 1944, King Mihai I staged a coup d'état with the army and ended Antonescu's dictatorship. Romania changed sides and declared war on Nazi Germany.

The dictator Antonescu was a close associate of Adolf Hitler. On May 17, 1946, he was executed as a war criminal. Romania remained a monarchy even after entering the Soviet sphere of influence. On December 30, 1947, the communist government forced King Mihai I to abdicate. The monarchy was dissolved and the Socialist Republic of Romania was established.

The nationalists from the AUR and the PSD do not want to admit that during the Antonescu era over 250,000 Romanian Jews were murdered by the „Iron Guard". Also in Northern Transylvania, which had fallen to Hungary, 120,000 Jews were murdered by the Hungarians.

At the beginning of World War II, the so-called Vienna Arbitration Awards of 1938 and 1940 were decided by Nazi Germany in favor of Hungary: The Trianon Treaty of 1920 was corrected. The northern part of Transylvania with Cluj-Napoca fell to Hungary and the southern part to Romania. Since 1945, the Treaty of Trianon has again been in force. During the Ceauşescu dictatorship, Romanians of Hungarian origin were not allowed to teach history and geography.

Romania always wanted to be on the winning side and therefore changed sides in the middle of the war. Our „friend and supporter" of today is our enemy of tomorrow. Is this a strategic decision or pure opportunism?

Tensions existed between Romania and Hungary even while both states were anchored in the Eastern Bloc. These tensions persist to this day. Since 2008, there has been a Trianon Research Institute in Budapest, which publishes under the title „Historical Magazine of Hungary." Similarly, the Greater Romania Party in Romania publishes a magazine. The membership in the EU, which does not allow any changes in the borders, has managed to prevent the nationalists in Hungary and Romania from starting a war.

3) How do you and your friends assess Romania's political situation today?

After the bachelor's degree, I immediately moved to Luxembourg, where I had already worked during my semester breaks. Many of my colleagues went home to their parents in Romania: There, the TV was on all day, as it is for all Romanians with little education. My parents raised me to be independent, which is rarely the case in Romanian families. Mostly the father and the mother decide and the children have to obey.

During the vacation I went to Timișoara , to visit my parents and friends. For my friends, the state is responsible for everything. I tried to explain to them that they themselves are responsible for their own lives, which they don't want to hear. They don't want to hear that the Romanian Parliament is the reflection of Romanian society.

My old colleagues can't or don't want to classify Romania properly, which has to do with Romanian history.

Economically weak nations, like all the Balkan countries, are not decision makers and do not play a role globally. In an economic country comparison of 80 countries, Romania ranks 68th, 49th in innovation, 47th in PISA ranking and 55th in business ranking. Fitch ranking: sometimes neutral, sometimes negative.

In terms of innovations in Romania during the Ceaușescu era, the country ranked 89th. Today, it is 49th in the ranking.

Arab states produce hardly any innovation and their universities play no role internationally. Religious fanaticism and religious extremism are responsible for the desolate situation for education and research.

If a country like Romania is dependent on financial benefits, especially from EU countries, and cannot defend itself either, then it is a very limited state. Its ranking is always down.

Millions of capable Romanians have left the country since 1990. They do not want to live in a country where networks and clans decide on advancement and promotions.

In Romania, it is still not important what you can do, but who you know. Superiors in management positions prefer to surround themselves with incompetent but compliant employees so that their own position is secure until retirement. This is especially the case in all state administrations.

My friends believe that with a master's degree they are entitled to appropriate jobs. That's how it was with Ceaușescu.

During the Ceaușescu era, Romania's industrial enterprises were mainly run by incompetent party bigwigs. That is why Romania and Bulgaria were the economic „bottom performers" of the former Eastern bloc countries.

Many Romanians assume that they will continue to receive financial support. In the meantime, Romania has been receiving support, especially from the EU, for 32 years. In a few years, Romania will go from being a financial recipient state to a financial donor state. That is, countries such as Northern Macedonia, Montenegro, Serbia, Bosnia-Herzegovina, and Albania will need to be supported, as will many countries in Africa. Donor countries (Scandinavia, Netherlands, Germany, Austria, France, etc...) enjoy a different status than receiving countries (Poland, Hungary, Slovakia, Czech Republic, Romania and Bulgaria).

Industrialized or developing country?

Romania is both. It is an industrialized country but at the same time a developing country. Many children have no real home. Lack of education and broken families are the biggest problem.

The country is rich in mineral resources, natural gas, hard coal, bauxite, etc.... Switzerland has no mineral resources at all. Nevertheless, with only 8.6 million inhabitants, Switzerland ranks 19th in the world with an export value of 380 billion euros per year. The reason for this is „human capital", a functioning democracy and a functioning legal system.

Trading volume:
USA Export: 1,750 billion US dollars
German exports worldwide: 1,376 billion euros
Romania Export worldwide: 56 billion euros
Germany's export is 25 times larger than Romania's. The USA's share in world trade is 10%, Germany's share is 7.62% and Romania's share in world trade is 0.3%.

Debt level:
USA: 31,000 billion euros
Germany: 2,300 billion euros
Switzerland: 109 billion euros
Romania: 133 billion euros
Romania's debt level compared to the USA: The USA has around 250 times as much debt as Romania. The exporting countries USA (No.1) and Germany (No.3) have a different ranking than Romania because they have a functioning democracy, a functioning legal system and a functioning market economy.

BIBLIOGRAPHY

- Adameșteanu , G.: Das Provisorium der Liebe, Berlin 2021
- Almond, M.: Decline without Fall. Romania without Ceaușescu , in: Frost, G.; Europe in Turmoil, Twickenham 1991
- Arendt, Hannah: Über die Revolution, Frankfurt am Main 1968
- Aida, J.: Erinnerung an die Deportation von Rumäniendeutschen in die UdSSR. Ein europäisches Erbe, in: Deutsche Welle vom 17.2.20202
- Behr, Edward: Kiss the hand that cannot bite – The life and death of the Ceaușescus, Hamish Mahilton 1991
- Beyme, Klaus von: Systemwechsel in Osteuropa, Frankfurt am Main 1994
- Bischof, Henrik: Am Vorabend der ersten freien Wahlen in Rumänien, Bonn 1990
- Bognar, P.: Beziehung zwischen Rumänien und Ungarn, in: Ost-West-Europäische, 4/2004
- Brandsch, K. R.: Flucht aus dem Reich Ceaușescus. 40 km im Fluss Timiș, Aachen 2004
- Braniste Lavinia, Sonja meldet sich, Berlin 2021
- Brown, James F.: Eastern Europe and Communist Rule, Durham, London 1988
- Brown, James F.: Nationalism, Democracy and Security in the Balkans, Aldershot 1992
- Brucan, Silviu: Pluralism and Social Conflict. A Social Analysis of the Communist World, New York 1990
- Brzezinski, Zbigniew: The Great Failure. The Birth and Death of Communism in the Twentieth Century, New York 1990
- Castellan, Georges: A History of the Romanians, Boulder 1989
- Ceaucescu, E.: Carnets Secrets, Flammarion 1990

- Ceaușescu, N.: The Genius of the Carpathians; Filiquariam Publishing, București 2008
- Cipkowski, Peter: Revolution in Eastern Europe. Understanding the Collapse of Communism in Poland, Hungary, East Germany, Czechoslovakia, Romania and the Sovjet Union, New York 1991
- Courtois, S.: Werth, N.; Louis J.; Panne, J. L.; Paczkowski, A.; Bartosek, K.; Margolin, J.-L.; Gauck, J.; Neubert, E.: Das Schwarzbuch des Kommunismus – Unterdrückung, Verbrechen und Terror -, Piper Verlag, München 2004
- Dahrendorf, R.: Betrachtungen über die Revolution in Europa, Stuttgart 1990
- Deletant, D.: Romania under Communist Rule, Civic Academy Foundation 1998
- Rumänien verärgert Russland mit Barbarossa, in: Die Welt, 29. September 2011
- Rumänien: Rechtsextreme Randale gegen deutschen Bürgermeister, in: Deutsche Welle vom 17.1.2022
- Essen von, Louisa: Das Schweigen einer Generation, in: Länderfokus vom 21.1.2021
- Experiente Carcerale in Romania Comunista; Institutul de Investigare a Crimelor Comunismului in Romania și Memoria Exilului Românesc
- Gabanyi, A. U.: Die unvollendete Revolution. Rumänien zwischen Diktatur und Demokratie, München 1990
- Gabanyi, A. U.: Systemwechsel in Rumänien. Von der Revolution zur Transformation, München 1989
- Galloway, George/Wylie, Bob: Downfall. The Ceaușescus and the Romanian Revolution, 1991

- Gilbert, Trond: Nationalism and Communism in Romania. The Rise and Fall of Ceaușescus Personal Dictatorship, Boulder 1990
- Gorczyca, M.: Diesseits und Jenseits des Tunnels 1945, Sibiu 2020
- Havel, Vaclev: Die unvollendete Revolution. Ein Gespräch mit Adam Michnik, in: Transit 4, 1992, S. 12-13
- Heinen, A.: Rumänien, der Holocaust und die Logik der Gewalt, Verlag Oldenburg, München 2007
- Janku, P.: Moskaus Feind ist der Westen, in: DW vom 19.5.2022
- Juchler, Jakob: Osteuropa im Umbruch. Politische, wirtschaftliche und gesellschaftliche Entwicklungen 1989-1993. Gesamtüberblick und Fallstudien, Zürich 1994
- Koenen, G.: Was war der Kommunismus?, Vandenhoeck, Göttingen 2010
- Laignel-Lavastine, Alexandra: „Le poids du nationalisme dans la transition roumaine", in: L'autre Europe 24/25, 1992, S. 110-132
- Laquer, Wlater: Die Intellektuellen und das Ende des Kommunismus, in: Europäische Rundschau, 1992, S. 87-92
- Lazu, C.: Maramuresch. Das Land der Holzkunst und der lebendigen Tradition, Sighet 2018
- Le Monde, 22.2.1997
- MDR Nachrichten vom 18. Februar 2021: In den Westen abgesetzt. Rumäniens bekanntester Geheimagent ist tot.
- Merrit, Giles: Eastern Europe and the USSR. The Challenge of Freedom, Brüssel 1991
- Olschewski, M.: Der Conducător – Phänomen der Macht, Wien 1990
- Oschlies, Wolf: Rumänien: Viele Veränderungen, keine Reformen, in: Bundesinstitut für Ostwissenschaftliche und internationale Stu-

dien (Hrsg.): Zwischen Krise und Konsolidierung. Gefährdeter Systemwechsel im Osten Europas, München 1995

- Pabst, V.: Die Nato hat die gefährdete Südost Flanke lange stiefmütterlich behandelt, in: NZZ vom 11.12.2021
- Pabst, V.: National, religiös und selbstbewusst gegenüber der EU: Rumäniens Rechtspopulisten blicken nach Polen, in: NZZ, 13.2.2021
- Pabst, V.: Rumäniens Präsident Klaus Johannis trat als Retter des Rechtsstaats ein. Von dieser Rolle bleibt nicht viel, in: NZZ vom 29.11.2021
- Papepa Ion Mihai Lt. Gen., Red Horizons; Regenery Gateway
- Rador, Antonia: Die Verschwörung der Securitate. Rumäniens verratene Revolution, Hamburg 1990
- Rank, H., Schlenk, J.: Ex-Präsident Ion Iliescu vor Gericht: Revolutionär oder Verbrecher?, Adenauerstiftung online, 30. Dezember 2019
- Rau, Milan: Die letzten Tage der Ceaușescus, Berlin 2010
- Remington, Thomas F. (Hrsg.): Parliament in Transition. The New Legislative Politics in the former USSR and Eastern Europe. Boulder 1994
- Scherr, K.; Gräf, R.: Rumänien, Geschichte und Geographie, Böhlau Verlag, Wien 2008
- Schmitt, O. J., Kirche und Wissenschaft bedrohen mit ihrer nationalorthodoxen Ideologie Rumäniens Westbindung, in: NZZ vom 26.10.2021
- Ein Kommentar von Dr. Christian Schuster, in Research Lab Democracy and Society in Transition: Die Parlamentswahlen in Rumänien 2020, 23.12.2020

- Tismaneanu, V.: Sieger oder Verlierer: Das moralische Dilemma der Osteuropäischen Intellektuellen, in: Osteuropäische Rundschau 4 (1992), S. 99-106
- Tismaneanu, V.: Stalinism for all Seasons – A Political History of Romanian Comunism, University of California Press, Berkeley 2003
- Elena Udrea: Vor Haftangriff abgetaucht und geschnappt, in: Romania Insider, 8. April 2022

PUBLICATIONS OF PROF. DR. DR. JOHANNES KNEIFEL

Die Kosten im Luftverkehr, München 1966.

Der Wettbewerb im nordatlantischen Luftverkehr – eine Untersuchung der Wettbewerbsverhältnisse und Wettbewerbsfaktoren, München 1968.

Accidents causés par les volées d'oiseaux, in: Revue Générale de l'Air, 25. Jg., 1969, Nr. 4, 1969.

L'Aviation Civile en République Démocratique Allemande, in: Revue Générale de l'Air, 33. Jg., Nr. 2, 1970, S. 158-174.

Die Zivilluftfahrt der Deutschen Demokratischen Republik – Eine Untersuchung der Entwicklung des Luftrechts der Zivilluftfahrt der DDR seit 1949 und ihre rechtlichen und wirtschaftlichen Beziehungen zu den COMECON-Fluggesellschaften, München 1970.

L'Aviation Civile en République Populaire de Chine, in: Revue Générale de l'Air, 35. Jg., Nr. 3, 1971, S.253-266.

Les Négociations relatives au transport aérien entre la R.F.A. et l'URSS, in: Revue Générale de l'Air, 35. Jg., Nr. 2, 1972, S. 166-173.

L'Aviation Civile en République Démocratique Allemande – Une étude de l'évolution de L'Aviation Civile et du droit aérien de la R.D.A. depuis 1949 et ses rapports juridiques et économiques avec les compagnies aériennes des Etats du COMECON et d'autres pays, Aix-Marseille 1970, Berlin-West 1972.

Air Transportation in Central America, Berlin-West 1972.

Air Laws of the European Countries (Lecture at the Faculty of Law, University of Seoul/Korea, 12.1.1972), Berlin-West 1972.

European Airlines – Present Situation and future outlook (Lecture at the Faculty of Economics, Tokio/Japan, 14.3.1972), Berlin-West 1972

Mongolflot, Compagnie aérienne de Mongolie, in: Revue Générale de l'Air, 35.Jg., 1972, Nr. 3.

Die Zivilluftfahrt der DDR und die Problematik des Berliner Luftverkehrs, in: Association Suisse de Droit Aérien et Spatial – Bulletin, Nr. 3, 1973.

World Directory of Civil Aviation Institutes and Governmental Civil Aviation Departments, Berlin-West 1973.

Rétrospective sur l'origine du droit d'accès des quatre puissances à Berlin par la voie des airs, in: Revue Générale de l'Air, Nr. 2, 1973.

Le Problème du Transport Aérien à Berlin et les Possibilités d'une nouvelle Réglementation, in: Revue Française des Droit Aérien, 36. Jg., Nr. 2, 1973, S. 162-181.

Le Développement de la Navigaton Aérienne Civile en République Populaire de Chine, in: Revue Française des Droit Aérien, 27. Jg., 1973, S. 261-283.

Les accords avec d'autres états ainsi que les tâches et la position de la compagnie aérienne CAAC, in: Revue Française des Droit Aérien, 27. Jg., 1973, S.261-283.

The Seagoing commerce of the German Democratic Republic, in: Scandinavian Shipping Gazette, Vol. 57, No 9, Okt. 1973.

La Compagnie Aérienne LOFTLEIDIR, Compagnie Non-IATA, in: Schweizerisches Archiv für Verkehrswissenschaft und Verkehrspolitik, 28. Jg., Nr. 3, S. 240-245.

Air Transportation to Berlin: past, present and future, in: Tijdschrift voor Vevoerswetenschap – Magazine for Transportation Science (Niederlande), Nr. 3, 1974, S. 159-177.

Air Laws and Treaties of the COMECON-States, 4 Bände, 1659 Seiten, Berlin-West 1974. Le transport aérien de marchandises en URSS, in: Il Diritto Aereo, 13. Jg., 1974, Nr. 51.

Bruits causés par les avions – Législation et mise en application en République Démocratique Allemande, in: Revue Française de Droit Aérien, 28. Jg., Heft 3, 1974.

La Route aérienne Sibérienne, in: Revue Générale de l'Air, 37. Jg., S. 122-125.

Aviation Laws of Central America – Analysis and Comparison to Aviation Laws of Western-Europe, Berlin-West 1974.

Der Berliner Luftverkehr mit besonderer Betrachtung der Entstehung der Zugangsrechte der Westmächte und Möglichkeiten einer Neuordnung, Berlin-West 1974.

Die Zivilluftfahrt der Volksrepublik China – Rückblick und Ausblick, Berlin 1975. German Civil Aviation Policy, Berlin-West 1975.

Air mail transport in the USSR, in: Il Diritto Aereo, 14. Jg, Nr. 55-56, Rom 1975.

La mise en service d'avions géants et de Jets par les pays du COMECON, in: Il Diritto Aereo, 14. Jg, Nr. 55-56, Rom 1975

Antragsverfahren zur Genehmigung von Landrechten beim Civil Aeronautics Board der USA am Beispiel der Fluggesellschaften Aeroflot, Tarom, LOT, CSA und JAT, in: Zeitschrift für Luft- und Weltraumrecht, 25. Jg., Heft 4, Dez. 1976, S. 323-338.

Lois Aériennes et Accords des Etats du COMECON, in: Revue Française de Droit Aérien, Nr. 2, 1976, S. 193-218.

A Study on the Choice of International Transportation – Cars, Trains, Planes – its Assessment and Synthesis, with special regard to sociological Aspects, Berlin-West 1976.

Stand und Ausbildung des im Luftverkehr der COMECON-Staaten beschäftigten Personals, in: Schweizerische Zeitschrift für Verkehrswirtschaft, 32. Jg., Nr. 2, Juni 1977.

Planung und Steuerung der Luftverkehrspolitik der COMECON-Staaten, in: Internationales Verkehrswesen, 29. Jg., Heft 3, Mai/Juni 1977, S. 151-158.

Zivilluftfahrt der Deutschen Demokratischen Republik – Luftfahrtsabkommen der DDR-Liniendienste der Interflug mit COMECON und Nicht-COMECON-Staaten – Interline – und Generalverkaufsagenturabkommen der Interflug, in: Zeitschrift für Luftund Weltraumrecht, 26. Jg., Heft 3, August 1977.

Market Research, planning and organizational Structures of the COMECON-airlines with special analysis of the air carrier „Interflug" of the German Democratic Republic, in: Air Law, Vol. 3, No. 2, 1978, S. 108-114.

Tarifgestaltung, Kosten und Rentabilität der COMECONFluggesellschaften am Beispiel der Interflug, in: Österreichische Verkehrs-Annalen, 25. Jg., 1. Heft, 1978, S. 20-33.

Luftverkehr im COMECON – mit Schwerpunkt DDR, München 1978.

Staatliches und internationales Luftverkehrsrecht der sozialistischen Staaten UdSSR, DDR, Polen, CSSR, Ungarn, Bulgarien, Rumänien und Jugoslawien, Nördlingen 1980.

Fluggesellschaften und Luftverkehrssysteme der sozialistischen Staaten UdSSR, Polen, CSSR, Ungarn, Bulgarien, Rumänien, Kuba, Jugoslawien und der VR China, Nördlingen 1980.

Aviation Laws of Bulgaria, the People's Republic of China, the CSSR, the German Democratic Republic, Hungary, the Democratic People's Republic of Korea, Laos, Poland, Romania, the USSR, Yugoslavia and the Republic of Vietnam, Vol. 1-6, 3926 pages, München 1980.

Civil Aviation of California, München 1985.

Bilateral Aviation Agreements of Mauritius and a comparison between the Mauritian Civil Aviation Act of 1974 and the Civil Aviation Regulations of the Federal Republic of Germany, Nördlingen 1989.

Internationales Verkehrswesen: Luftverkehr, Flughäfen, Eisenbahn, Binnen- und Hochseeschifffahrt, Straßenverkehr, Logistik und Rohrleitungsverkehr, München, 2010

Eine Reise in Bildern durch meine 82 Jahre, München 2021